THE ECONOMICS OF JOHN MAYNARD KEYNES

Widely recognized as one of the greatest economists in history, there has been a surge of interest in the work of John Maynard Keynes since the financial crisis of 2008 with people looking for solutions to rebalance the economy. Presciently, Keynes argued that free markets are unable to fully organize economic activity and that the steadying and reforming hand of the State is needed for capitalism to function properly. In the aftermath of the financial crisis of 2008, exacerbated by a global pandemic, these ideas are more timely than ever.

This book provides an introduction to Keynes' thoughts on capitalism, the State, and macroeconomics. It starts with Keynes' epistemological theory of his *A Treatise on Probability* (1921), from which aspects such as uncertainty and the decision-making process, both later important in his economic work, can be drawn. The book then pursues Keynes' economic writings. From *A Tract on the Monetary Reform* (1923) and *A Treatise on Money* (1930), it shows Keynes' pursuit of a full understanding of the role of money in the economy. Keynes masterfully demonstrated the knowledge he gained through his 1936 masterpiece *The General Theory of Employment, Interest and Money*. Going beyond Keynes' classic, this book also explores his later work on economic policy prescriptions and finally his concept of State and economic development.

This accessible introduction to the economic thought of Keynes will be essential reading for those interested in the history and development of economics, as well as political scientists, sociologists, historians, and others seeking an overview of these foundational economic ideas.

Fabio Terra was born in Araxa, a town in the state of Minas Gerais, Brazil. He received a Bachelor of Economics degree from the Federal University of Uberlandia, an MSc degree from the Federal University of Parana, and a PhD degree from the Federal University of Rio Grande do Sul. He is a professor at the Federal University of ABC and of the Post-graduate Program in Economics of the Federal University of Uberlandia, as well as a researcher at the Brazilian Council for Scientific and Technological Development. He is Former Visiting Fellow of Wolfson College, University of Cambridge, UK, and Former Chair of the Brazilian Keynesian Association.

THE ECONOMICS OF JOHN MAYNARD KEYNES

Fabio Terra

Routledge
Taylor & Francis Group

LONDON AND NEW YORK

Designed cover image: © Getty Images

First published 2023
by Routledge
4 Park Square, Milton Park, Abingdon, Oxon OX14 4RN

and by Routledge
605 Third Avenue, New York, NY 10158

Routledge is an imprint of the Taylor & Francis Group, an informa business

© 2023 Fabio Terra

British Library Cataloguing-in-Publication Data
A catalogue record for this book is available from the British Library

ISBN: 978-1-032-26211-6 (hbk)
ISBN: 978-1-032-26210-9 (pbk)
ISBN: 978-1-003-28709-4 (ebk)

DOI: 10.4324/9781003287094

Typeset in Bembo
by Apex CoVantage, LLC

To my beloved parents Iolivan and Eliane

To my loved sweetest thing, Fernanda

*To my dear masters, Fernando Ferrari Filho
and Fernando Cardim de Carvalho*

To all those who believe in a better world, just like you do

CONTENTS

ACKNOWLEDGMENTS

I am grateful to all my professors for the knowledge they have kindly given to me. I am also thankful to Brazilian State for all the education and financial grants it has provided me with. I hope I am returning it back to the Brazilian society in the classes I lecture as well as in the research I do, of which this book is the most important work I have done so far.

INTRODUCTION

John Maynard Keynes was the greatest economist of the 20th century. His legacy to economics is such that there are a few theoretical perspectives carrying the surname Keynesian to qualify their names: Neoclassical Keynesian Synthesis, Post Keynesian, and New Keynesian. Although these theories have Keynes in their surnames and they all descend from some readings of his work, they are not one single family and even less carry a unique understanding of his economics. The only common point within this great diversity of perspectives emerging from one single author is how influent this author is.

This book, *The Economics of John Maynard Keynes*, aims to present the economic theory of this magnificent author in a straightforward and simple manner. There is an ongoing interest in Keynes' economic theory not only from the academic public but also from the non-academic public interested in economics and finance. But Keynes wrote his major theoretical economic works without directly talking to the general public. His intention was to debate with and defeat the mainstream economics of his time, namely, neoclassical economics. Thus, reading Keynes' economics, especially his masterpiece *The General Theory of Employment, Interest and Money*, is not always an easy job. This book intends to facilitate the task and translate Keynes' economics to all those interested in his work.

Keynes published his 1936 masterpiece, *The General Theory*, late in his life, just ten years before his death in 1946. He did not come to this book in a once and for all manner. He changed his ideas over time, in a constant struggle to liberate himself from the economics he had been taught in the University of Cambridge and that later he lectured there for years. In this book, we follow this winding road Keynes hit to develop an economics of his own. We start with his 1921 *A Treatise on Probability*. Although economics was not the topic of this book, it offers a very interesting insight into how Keynes saw human reasoning and decision-making processes, which helps to understand *A Treatise on Money* and *The General Theory*.

DOI: 10.4324/9781003287094-1

After that, we follow the road Keynes travelled in his journey in economics. The first stop is at Keynes' 1923 *A Tract on Monetary Reform* and the second at the 1930 *A Treatise on Money*. Then we arrive at *The General Theory*.

In *A Tract on Monetary Reform*, Keynes aimed to explain inflation, which was razing Central Europe in the beginning of the 1920s. In *A Treatise on Money*, he was still interested in explaining prices but now their dynamics of both inflation and deflation. Then, in our presentation of those two books, we will focus on Keynes' explanation of the causes of price variations and the role of money in these. Our passage through both books will be brief: a chapter for each book. Our stop in these two books is short due to our main interest be *The General Theory*, at which our journey will have several stops aiming to explain Keynes' masterpiece in detail. We take *The General Theory* as the synthesis of Keynes' pursuit to deliver a totally new economic theory. After *The General Theory*, we describe the economic policy proposals that Keynes made as well as his notion of State and development.

In view of that, we deliver an organic view of Keynes' economics – that is, his work throughout his life is taken as an effort to arrive at *The General Theory*. However, this organic reading of Keynes, which recalls and reports the evolution of his economic thoughts over time, does not mean that his ideas had no ruptures. Keynes changed the course of his thoughts many times with a fearless tendency to surpass his discomforts with both the economic theory of his time and his own attempts to solve what bothered him. Therefore, consistency in this book means Keynes' unstoppable search for an economic model that answered the questions he raised and not an unbreakable linear thought evolution throughout his life.

We do not desire to furnish a final account of Keynes' economics in this book. Far from that, our intention is to explain his economics in an easy manner for those interested in the topic, including those outside the academy. Themes other than Keynes' economics, such as the controversies among those who interpreted his works, deep details of his biography, the Bloomsbury group, his role at the Versailles Conference or at Bretton Woods, will not be regarded in this book. Moreover, it is not the purpose of this book to present and discuss Post Keynesian economics, whose affiliated authors have been recalling and advancing the work of Keynes for decades. There are several great books on Post Keynesian economics, whereas books on Keynes' economics are rather scarce, if not in absolute terms, at least when compared to the continuous existing interest in Keynes. Thus, there is room for more on Keynes' economics itself, and this book helps in addressing this gap.

All in all, this book focuses on the economics of Keynes. It intends to be almost a kind of, say, pocket-handbook through which readers understand Keynes and to which they call upon whenever they have doubts about some aspect of his thinking. The chapters of the book are short and bring a digested explanation of Keynes' economics. The book is meant to be very concise, without digressions or presentations of other authors and theories, and extremely centered on Keynes' own writings. When it improves the comprehension of his theory, the book briefly takes all necessary dialogues with other authors, theories, and history. In this sense, the road Keynes traveled in his economic works led him off neoclassical theory and he struggled to get rid of neoclassical influence. Hence, whenever it makes Keynes' thoughts clear, we compare them with those of neoclassical theory.

This book has four parts. Part I, Foundations, recalls Keynes' *A Treatise on Probability* to describe the origins of uncertainty and outline how individuals make decisions under uncertainty. *In The General Theory*, decision under unavoidable uncertainty is a key element, and *A Treatise on Probability* furnishes a good ground to understand uncertainty and its consequences on decision-making. Chapter 2 briefly presents a very much controversial topic to Keynesianism in general: method. Nevertheless, the book has a position on the theme, inspired by *A Treatise on Probability*.

Part II, Flirting with Money, has two chapters. They cover how Keynes treated money in *A Tract on Monetary Reform* and *A Treatise on Money*, respectively. The intention is to report how Keynes started his quest to understand money and its role in the economy differently from neoclassical economics. Notwithstanding his will for writing a theory of his own, in these two books, Keynes was still somewhat attached to other schools of thought. In *A Tract on Monetary Reform*, approached in Chapter 3, Keynes developed his own quantity theory of money, but he believed that the original money quantity theory was valid in the long term. In *A Treatise on Money*, explained in Chapter 4, we will see a Wicksellian Keynes, in which Keynes' monetary theory was influenced by the Swede economist Knut Wicksell.

Keynes' full mindset shift happened with his *The General Theory*, explained in detail throughout the eight chapters (Chapters 5–12) of Part III – Keynes' checkmate: *The General Theory of Employment, Interest and Money*. It was with *The General Theory* that Keynes bequeathed his surname to economics: he finally developed his own economic tradition. It is not time for spoilers, so the tip to catch your attention is letting you know that in *The General Theory* Keynes made no concession to neoclassical economics nor to Knut Wicksell; he developed a theory of production and no longer saw price as the variable that economics should chiefly explain; he started seeing full employment as a very much rare economic situation; he created an economic theory in which economic activity is pushed by the demand side of the economy. Furthermore, in *The General Theory*, Keynes reached his eureka about money.

Part III is structured as follows. Chapter 5 explains how Keynes checkmated neoclassical theory and its supply-side economics. Chapter 6 describes Keynes' effective demand principle to explain the demand-side economics. If demand pushes the dynamics of the economy, we then explain the components of demand. Chapter 7 discloses *The General Theory's* theory of consume, while Chapter 8 accounts for the investment theory. Then it is time to consider money and its relationship with demand. Chapter 9 exposes the liquidity preference theory from which the interest rate theory emerges. Chapter 10 explains why money is so special in the economic system; thereby, it reveals how Keynes clarified money's special properties. Chapter 11 synthesizes *The General Theory,* while Chapter 12 goes through other important topics of the book such as prices, wages, and trade cycles.

Part IV of the book – Beyond *The General Theory* – depicts both Keynes' economic policy proposals and notions of State and development. Keynes is well known for being a great proposer of State economic action, and quite often it is heard and read that his motions for economic policing, especially those regarding fiscal policy, are to be found in *The General Theory*. However, this is not the case. Apart from monetary policy, whose Keynes' prescriptions can be seen in *The General Theory* (as well as in *A Treatise on Money* and other texts), it is not in Keynes' masterpiece that you will find the great deal of his economic policy proposals. We display them in Part IV.

Hence, Chapter 13 details Keynes' proposals for fiscal policy; Chapter 14 talks about monetary policy; and Chapter 15 depicts the exchange rate policy. If States make economic policy and if Keynes deemed their economic action as especially important to the social and economic progresses, thus Chapter 16 characterizes Keynes' notion of the State. Finally, Chapter 17 develops Keynes' notion of economic development, seen as the final step toward which his economic theory and economic policy prescriptions were meant to lead. At the developed stage of society, Keynes hoped that economic problems would no longer be the greatest issues troubling humankind, as they have been for centuries and remain to be the case.

Before delving into *The Economics of John Maynard Keynes*, let us clarify the following. You will have the best knowledge of Keynes' economics if you read this whole book. The book's chapters are concise, and the language used on them is simple to make it easier for you to keep your attention while reading. But, despite our effort to make this book a digested peruse of Keynes, Parts I and II might seem a bit abstract. Thus, if you are interested in acquainting only the core of Keynes' economics, it will be no problem if you go straight to Parts III and IV. Lest you now that if you decide to skip Parts I and/or II, you will lose very nice content about Keynes, but you will not be bereft of what is essential to understand his economics. Be welcome to *The Economics of John Maynard Keynes*.

References

Keynes, J. M. (1921). *A Treatise on Probability*. London: Macmillan.

Keynes, J. M. (2013a). *A Tract on Monetary Reform: The Collected Writings of John Maynard Keynes*, vol. IV. London: Cambridge University Press.

Keynes, J. M. (2013b). *A Treatise on Money I, the Pure Theory of Money: The Collected Writings of John Maynard Keynes*, vol. V. London: Cambridge University Press.

Keynes, J. M. (2013c). *A Treatise on Money II, the Applied Theory of Money: The Collected Writings of John Maynard Keynes*, vol. VI. London: Cambridge University Press.

Keynes, J. M. (2013d). *The General Theory of Employment, Interest and Money: The Collected Writings of John Maynard Keynes*, vol. VII. London: Royal Economic Society and Cambridge University Press.

PART I
Foundations

Although *A Treatise on Probability* was published in 1921, Keynes drafted this book a decade before, in the second half of the 1900s. It is a book on probability, but Keynes discussed several topics in it rather than solely probability. He entered the fields of epistemology and logic, always rooting his arguments on strong philosophical and mathematical bases. While debating probability, Keynes developed an epistemological theory in which uncertainty is an inescapable feature of human knowledge that is necessarily embedded in individual decision-making processes. Keynes also broadly debated the method of knowledge in *A Treatise on Probability*.

In this book, we assume that *A Treatise on Probability* grounds founding elements of Keynes' economics, namely, uncertainty, decision-making processes, and method. They are foundations because they bear the epistemological and methodological bases that support Keynes' economics, especially, but not only, in *The General Theory*. Uncertainty, decision-making processes, and the method of knowledge are explained in the two chapters of this part. Chapter 1 approaches uncertainty and decision-making processes. Chapter 2 explores method.

But how is this related to Keynes' economics? In the first place, *A Treatise on Probability* helps to understand the origins of uncertainty, which is key in Keynes' economics. Second, it also permits us to outline a decision-making process model, which is helpful when we present the investment theory of *A Treatise on Money* and *The General Theory* chapters ahead. Finally, *A Treatise on Probability* also backs our argument about Keynes' method, which has a role to play in his economics, especially in *The General Theory*.[1]

Note

1 Continuity versus rupture in Keynes' thoughts is a hot topic in Post Keynesian theory. It is not the topic of this book though, so if you would like to learn more on that, see:

DOI: 10.4324/9781003287094-2

O'Donnel (1989, 2002), Bateman (1989, 1991), and Winslow (1986, 1989). Our position in this book is that Keynes changed some of his thoughts during his life, like his view on money, but he maintained others, especially those he had advanced in *A Treatise on Probability*. This position is also seen in Carvalho (1988, 1992, 2003).

References

Bateman, B. W. (1989). '"Human Logic" and Keynes' Economics: A Comment', *Eastern Economic Journal*, 15(1), pp. 63–67.

Bateman, B. W. (1991). 'Das Maynard Keynes Problem', *Cambridge Journal of Economics*, 15(1), pp. 100–111.

Carvalho, F. J. C. (1988). 'Keynes on Probability, Uncertainty and Decision Making', *Journal of Post-Keynesian Economics*, 11(1), pp. 66–81.

Carvalho, F. J. C. (1992). *Mr. Keynes and the Post Keynesians*. Cheltenham: Edward Elgar.

Carvalho, F. J. C. (2003). 'Características Essenciais do Método de Keynes na Teoria Geral', in Corazza, G. (ed.) *Métodos da Ciência Econômica*. Porto Alegre: UFRGS, pp. 175–188.

Keynes, J. M. (1921). *Treatise on Probability*. London: Macmillan.

Keynes, J. M. (2013b). *A Treatise on Money I, the Pure Theory of Money: The Collected Writings of John Maynard Keynes*, vol. V. London: Cambridge University Press.

Keynes, J. M. (2013c). *A Treatise on Money II, the Applied Theory of Money: The Collected Writings of John Maynard Keynes*, vol. VI. London: Cambridge University Press.

Keynes, J. M. (2013d). *The General Theory of Employment, Interest and Money: The Collected Writings of John Maynard Keynes*, vol. VII. London: Royal Economic Society and Cambridge University Press.

O'Donnel, R. M. (1989). *Keynes: Philosophy, Economics and Politics*. New York: St. Martin's Press.

O'Donnell, R. M. (2002). *The Thick and the Thin of Controversy: A Critique of Bateman on Keynes*. Research Papers 0204. Sydney: Macquarie University, Department of Economics.

Winslow, E. G. (1986). '"Human Logic" and Keynes' Economics', *Eastern Economic Journal*, 12(4), pp. 413–430.

Winslow, E. G. (1989). '"Human Logic" and Keynes' Economics: A Reply to Bateman', *Eastern Economic Journal*, 15(1), pp. 67–70.

1
THE ORIGINS OF UNCERTAINTY

How do you think? Set aside the biological and neurological aspects of the human brain for a moment. How do you form ideas about an object that awakes your curiosity? Epistemology deals with this issue, and Keynes was interested in promoting his own epistemological theory in *A Treatise on Probability*.

To Keynes, the first step of reasoning is direct acquaintance. Using innate senses, humans can understand, experience, and perceive. These three activities provide humans with the ability to acquire direct knowledge of things that then became known to individuals. It is not important to define the directly acquired knowledge as right or wrong. The key element here is that senses-based direct acquaintance builds the second step of reasoning, namely, direct knowledge (also called propositions or evidence).

This is a quite abstract matter; therefore, an example helps. People perceive the media daily broadcasting financial news, such as stock exchange indexes and interest rates, and learn that there are possible options for investing money. People directly acquainted with the media's reports understand things associated with financial investments that become direct knowledge to them. This process is surely not as monotonous as this instance suggests. It happens in multiple ways, with several elements being concomitantly sensed, thus acquired, and then acknowledged.

Direct knowledge grounds the third and last step of reasoning, indirect knowledge (also called conclusion or argument). From the set of direct knowledge, individuals try to reach new knowledge, which is something they do not know but that seems reasonable to conclude based on their direct knowledge. In other words, humans accumulate direct knowledge and use it to go further, attempting to learn something they do not yet know. This unknown thing, indirect knowledge, is the conclusion emerging from the reasoning process.

Let us return to our example. People who learned about financial investments have direct knowledge. They use this set of direct knowledge to generate the

DOI: 10.4324/9781003287094-3

indirect knowledge (i.e., they conclude) that financial investments, say, in equities of company X, are worth making. The conclusion is reasonable because it emerges from individuals' set of direct knowledge. But is this conclusion correct? We do not know yet. Only time will tell if company X's equities were profitable.

Keynes was not concerned with correctness, but with reasonableness. In *A Treatise on Probability*, he developed an epistemological theory to validate thoughts that could be wrong at the end of the day but whose reasoning processes, the thinking that led to them, were nevertheless reasonable. Keynes' message was that mistake does not mean irrationality, as he explained: "But is it certain that Newton and Huyghens were only reasonable when their theories were true, and that their mistakes were the fruit of a disordered fancy?" (Keynes, 1921, p. 284).

Indirect knowledge is a logical possibility, an expectation. It is not something that can be fully known when the conclusions are drawn. Shackle, in his 1979 *Imagination and Nature of Choice*, explained this by using the concept of figment of imagination. Conclusions are imaginative and constructed by thinkers while they think. Please do not consider imagination as being somehow undisciplined. Instead, take it in the sense of building clear-minded images in the pursuit of reasonable conclusions.

Indirect knowledge is concluded from the direct knowledge set. However, the former is not a component of the latter. Indirect knowledge is not known; it is not even more-or-less known. It is just an inkling imagined from acknowledged propositions. If indirect knowledge is unknown, it is always uncertain whether it is right or wrong. It is simply not possible to previously guarantee the certainty of indirect knowledge. Thus, it is always an expectation. Expectations are the unavoidable counterpart of uncertainty. Logically, if you are uncertain about your indirect knowledge, it can only be an expectation, a thought you expect to be true. Let us go back to our example. Buyers of company X's equities need to wait to determine if their expected conclusion of profiting was correct. When the decision to buy the equities was made, their future prices did not exist.

Where is probability in *A Treatise on Probability*? Keynes did not take probability as the usual quantitative relationship between the frequency of events. He stated that probability is the logical relationship between direct and indirect knowledge and that this relationship is not quantitatively measurable as it is in the frequentist tradition of probability. Thus, Keynes created a non-numerical subjective probability measure called the degree of rational belief.

This degree of rational belief, in turn, varies according to the weight of arguments. The meaning of this latter concept is controversial because Keynes did not define it in a unique manner. Hence, we side with Vercelli (2010) and present three definitions of the weight of arguments. The first is related to the *size* of the direct knowledge set from which indirect knowledge is drawn. The second refers to how much is assumed to be really known by holders of direct knowledge; in other words, the second definition of the concept is the answer you would give to the following question: how much do you *really* know of what you know? The third definition of the weight of arguments is associated with the comparison between the set of direct knowledge and the set of ignorance about an object. The set of direct knowledge is what individuals know about an object. The set of ignorance is evidence that individuals acknowledge as being important to understanding something, but they recognize that they are ignorant about this evidence; they do not know it. Individuals who judge their set of direct knowledge to be greater than their set of ignorance place greater weight on their argument, and vice versa.

Vercelli (2010) argued that these three definitions are complementary as they function in the same logical sense. The bigger the set of direct knowledge, the greater the proportion of what is assumed to be known. The larger the direct knowledge set compared to the ignorance set, the greater the weight of an argument. In conclusion, the greater the weight of an argument, the higher the degree of rational belief that individuals have in their indirect knowledge. This is Keynes' subjective probability.

Intuition and Induction

In Keynes' view, reasoning processes are full of intuition. This is illustrated by the notion of a *subjective* and *qualitative* degree of rational belief. Science, in general, and economics, in particular, leave no room for intuition in their theories. However, independent of the preferences of science and economics, intuition is an undeniable and important characteristic of humans. Thus, Keynes considered it in his epistemology and, of course, in his economics.

What is the method to develop knowledge – that is, what bridges direct knowledge and indirect knowledge? In Keynes' words, "inductive processes have formed, of course, at all times a vital, habitual part of the mind's machinery" (Keynes, 1921, p. 250). The inductive process, or simply induction, is the method of acquiring knowledge by combining particular evidence to form a general conclusion. In turn, induction as a mechanism of human reasoning means that individuals depart from particular direct knowledge to arrive at general indirect knowledge. Therefore, induction is the method by which humans think – thus, it is more than just a scientific tool. Moreover, if people think inductively, Keynes realized it would be crucial to adopt induction to understand economics. The next chapter further discusses this topic.

We are not yet into Keynes' economic theories, but uncertainty and expectations are well-known components of them. He advanced both concepts in *A Treatise on Money*, but it was in *The General Theory* that uncertainty and expectations became paramount. If you take uncertainty only from Keynes' masterpiece, *The General Theory*, you might see it as an assumption, a presupposition that Keynes made for theorizing his economics. However, uncertainty and expectations are inherent consequences of people thinking inductively, as Keynes explained "our knowledge . . . is often reached inductively, and shares the uncertainty to which all inductions are liable" (Keynes, 1921, p. 95). Induction intrinsically results in uncertain indirect knowledge, and as such, it can consist of nothing but expectations. Because of induction, uncertainty and its counterpart, expectations, are not presuppositions of Keynes' economics: they are outcomes of how people think.

Uncertainty is a consequence of the inductive processes by which humans think. In this sense, uncertainty is an epistemological characteristic of humans, whose knowledge capacity is always limited, independent of how large this capacity is. It does not exist a human being that can know everything about everything, especially when this everything includes things that do not yet exist, like the future. Furthermore, the environment strengthens the limits of human rationality because it cannot furnish all the information necessary to be directly known. There is always some evidence that is either non-existent or unavailable as restless social and natural dynamics continuously change the available evidence. The world is constantly destroying old evidence and constructing new material. Therefore, the direct knowledge set moves constantly, adding environmental uncertainty to the indelible epistemological uncertainty.

This is especially true when time causes the unknowable future to provide the moment revealing how correct a previously reached conclusion is. Take, for instance, your economic decisions: they are always enclosed by time, independent of which country you are in. Current outcomes arrive from past decisions; meanwhile, other decisions that are still being made today will only reveal their results in the future. As Carvalho (2003) taught, decisions, including the economic ones, do not simply wait for the future; in fact, they build it. Therefore, the future is the result of thousands of uncoordinated, unknowable, and contemporary decisions that individuals make. They make those decisions by inductively reasoning uncertain conclusions that they expect to be true based on their direct knowledge.

The Decision-Making Process

Keynes' epistemology enables us to outline a model of the decision-making process. Incidentally, scientists, including economists, use the term model quite often. When scientists explain phenomena (also called objects) in a theory, they offer a model. Models are simple explanations of the object. They are simple because phenomena are complex, with several determinants, and the conditions of their functioning vary with circumstances. Thus, it is impossible for researchers to replicate the object in all its detail. To take an analogy, fashion models do not present all the clothes of the season but instead exemplify the trends. Likewise, theoretical models intend to describe the general lines of how the object functions as well as the relevant variables to explain it and their relationship with it. Every time the word model appears in this book, this is what it means.

Our decision-making model starts with direct knowledge, which is evidence that individuals have and assume to know. Departing from direct knowledge, individuals use induction to generate indirect knowledge, which necessarily goes further than their set of direct knowledge. As indirect knowledge is not part of the direct knowledge set, it is always unknown; thus, the conclusion is necessarily uncertain. Induction generalizes an expected and unobserved conclusion from known (at least partially) particular evidence. Because conclusions can never be certain, they can be nothing but expectations of decision-makers.

For instance, a Brazilian entrepreneur knows that Brazilians like ice-cream a lot; maybe not as much as in Italy, but enough to secure demand. She is also cognizant of other information regarding Brazil, such as the minimum wage, GDP growth, unemployment level, interest rates, last year's ice-cream consumption, best-selling flavors, and other economic data. Non-economic information is also available; for example, the historical average temperature of each season is accessible and might be evidence good enough to infer the seasonality of demand.

The entrepreneur uses all these data to induce some indirect knowledge, by which we mean that she expects to profit by becoming an ice-cream producer and reckons that she will get richer than if she invests in financial assets, like equities of company X and bonds of the Brazilian Treasury. She also concludes that she had better produce several flavors because Brazilians have different tastes for ice-cream and that a good market strategy is to sell creative seasonal flavors, which might draw attention to her brand. She considers her thoughts reasonable and the weight of her arguments considerable. She has got a great degree of rational belief in her expectations. Thus, she invests; but only time will tell if her expectations, her indirect knowledge, are correct.

Shackle (1979) always remarked that when an investment decision effectively becomes an expenditure, the investment made is crucial: once money is spent to buy raw materials, equipment, and capital assets and to employ contractors and workers, the amount spent is gone forever from the entrepreneur's vault. The reason is time: it is irreversible, marching ever onward; there is no way to reset the game and restore the initial conditions. This is the type of time Keynes considered, which we call the historical or calendar time. In contrast, neoclassical economics and the schools of thought it later inspired, such as Monetarist, New Keynesian, and New Classical, considered time as only logical. As such, it is not historical or temporal; it does not run through clocks and calendars. Logical time is just a parameter that, at best, differentiates what should be understood as the short or long term.

We are still in *A Treatise on Probability*, but our example of a decision-making process already anticipated the entrepreneurial behavior that Keynes outlined in his *General Theory*. This is not a coincidence. It results from the consistent development of his thought over time. As this chapter closes, let us restate it using Keynes as an example. Keynes accumulated direct knowledge throughout his life so that he could induce with a greater degree of rational belief more complex indirect knowledge to the point that in 1936, late in his life, he generalized *The General Theory*. *A Treatise on Probability* is not a book on economics, but it helps us to understand Keynes' economics. Thus, we make another helpful stop in this book to talk about the method Keynes used. This is the topic of the next chapter.

References

Carvalho, F. J. C. (2003). 'Características Essenciais do Método de Keynes na Teoria Geral', in Corazza, G. (ed.) *Métodos da Ciência Econômica*. Porto Alegre: UFRGS, pp. 175–188.

Keynes, J. M. (1921). *A Treatise on Probability*. London: Macmillan.

Keynes, J. M. (2013b). *A Treatise on Money I, the Pure Theory of Money: The Collected Writings of John Maynard Keynes*, vol. V. London: Cambridge University Press.

Keynes, J. M. (2013c). *A Treatise on Money II, the Applied Theory of Money: The Collected Writings of John Maynard Keynes*, vol. VI. London: Cambridge University Press.

Keynes, J. M. (2013d). *The General Theory of Employment, Interest and Money: The Collected Writings of John Maynard Keynes*, vol. VII. London: Royal Economic Society and Cambridge University Press.

Shackle, G. L. S. (1979). *Imagination and the Nature of Choice*. Edinburgh: Edinburgh University Press.

Vercelli, A. (2010). *Weight of Argument and Economic Decisions*. Department of Economic Policy, Finance and Development (DEPFID) 0610. Siena: Department of Economic Policy, Finance and Development (DEPFID) of the Siena University.

2
A BRIEF DEBATE ABOUT A CONTROVERSIAL TOPIC

Keynes' Method

What is the scientific method? It is the tool that scientists use to approach phenomena, which are their objects of interest. Method is not a toll exclusive to scientists. In fact, it is how all individuals address the things they want to know or make. For example, when you cook something, all the steps as well as the kitchen utensils that the recipe requires are the method to approach and attain the object of interest, in this case, the dish. Throughout his major economic works, Keynes did not explicitly announce or discuss the method he used. However, as the author of a vast oeuvre, debates about his method arose and created controversies.

While this book shies away from this contentious debate, you can find further information about it in Terra and Ferrari Filho (2018). Nevertheless, we sustain a position about the method Keynes used in his economics: it was induction. We recognize that Keynes may pragmatically have used other approaches in his research; however, we will show throughout this book that induction played an extensive and key role in his economics.

In comparison, the method used by neoclassical economics was deduction. The classical economist David Ricardo, who was a fervent user of deduction and cemented it in economics, bequeathed this method to neoclassical economics. Followers of the neoclassical tradition today still use it, in the form of hypothetical deductive reasoning. Whenever deduction is in place, scientific inquiries start with stating abstract and general assumptions from which a particular conclusion is derived. The abstract and general assumptions launching a deductive process need not be observed or experienced. It is only required that they maintain logical consistency with a particular conclusion resulting from them. Milton Friedman's (1953) positivist view on the methodology of economics is present here. He stated that the realism of hypotheses is fully dismissible since models arising from abstract general presuppositions produce conclusions compatible with observed facts and furnish good predictions of phenomena.

DOI: 10.4324/9781003287094-4

There are big methodological differences between Keynes and the neoclassical tradition. Starting with the latter, since neoclassical economists use deduction, the assumption they set out to design how people behave becomes their expectations of the correct behavior of people. If for any reason people behave differently from what is presupposed, the theory will say that people are mistaken. By using deduction and declaring what *should be* the correct behavior of people, the neoclassical economists act as if they are sitting in an ivory tower to observe people but assuming that they are unrelated to these very people and capable of deciding what people's correct or incorrect behavior is (and which these theorists deem as rational and irrational, respectively).

In turn, Keynes had a different methodological approach. In the last chapter, we quoted his defense of induction as the method by which humans think. If induction is the method of human reasoning, it follows that it is also the method of Keynes' own reasoning. A quick historical digression illustrates how Keynes was preoccupied with theorizing based on people, as they truly are and not as his theory assumed or needed them to be. In *A Treatise on Probability*, Keynes criticized his Cambridge philosophy fellows Bertrand Russell and Ludwig Wittgenstein because of their use of formal language to structure and (especially) present their philosophy. Keynes saw it as pedantry because ordinary people use ordinary language in their everyday life and not formal language, and thus they could not easily understand Russell, Wittgenstein, and other philosophers.

As Carvalho (2003) originally explored, years after the young philosopher Keynes wrote *A Treatise on Probability*, the economist Keynes continued theorizing on behalf of ordinary people by putting himself in the shoes of people. Keynes looked at the world as people look at it. He thought of economics as people thought of it in their day-by-day life. Thus, in his economics, Keynes did not use formal language, despite it being math's language and Keynes had a bachelor's degree in mathematics. This explains why you will neither see speech structured in formal language nor long algebra derivations in his economic books.

Keynes' concern with using the method and the language of ordinary people was based on an ethical principle that drove his life as a scientist. This principle is the philosophy of practice. It states that the study and comprehension of things are not the end but the means to act and solve problems in the world. Keynes believed that theories were not for contemplation, but for promoting interventions and changes. This ethical behavior is illustrated by his indefatigable work with different British governments, his prolific academic life, and his arguing for State economic intervention throughout his economic works. Keynes deemed economics a moral science, that is, a scientific field whose objects inexorably emerge from human action. He intended his economics to become practical activities. Thus, he needed to begin by understanding how humans, the creators of the economy, think and behave. Keynes believed that induction could help in this task more than any other method.

Chapter 1 explained that induction is the inquiry that departs from individual evidence to arrive at a general conclusion. It was also shown that conclusions inductively reasoned are always uncertain because they are not components of the evidence set from which they were derived. As a result, induction conveys uncertainty, trial and error, ignorance, and unpredictability of the future, which are features confronting humans in their everyday lives. But neoclassical economics does not incorporate these features in its models. Keynes, disagreeing profoundly with this absence, thought that if uncertainty, trial and error, ignorance, and unpredictability of the future are features daily experienced by humans, they should be normal aspects of his economics, too.

In *A Treatise on Probability*, Keynes discussed induction carefully. He divided induction into two sub-methods, namely, analogy and pure induction. Analogy is the examination of an object by comparing its characteristics with those of another object to single out similarities and differences between the compared objects. There are two kinds of analogy, positive and negative. In the first, objects have similar singular features, whereas, in the latter, they do not resemble each other. In turn, pure induction is the accumulation of observed and experienced singular evidence from which a general conclusion is inferred. Pure induction is what is usually taken for induction, but Keynes went further and developed analogy as a component of induction as well.[1]

The larger the objects compared by positive and negative analogies and the larger the pure induction set of experienced and observed evidence, the greater the agents' weight of arguments and the more confidently they induce a general conclusion about something they strive to know. Among these agents are ordinary people as well as the scientist John Maynard Keynes, to whom the comprehension of how people truly reason was crucial for outlining his economics. If people think inductively, then so should scientists while researching an object; this is what Keynes did when theorizing his economics.

Analogy expands the power of inductive inferences relative to the sole use of pure induction because it permits the discovery and accumulation of singular evidence from abstract non-observable particular events. Thereby, analogy makes it possible to compare intangible objects like theories, hypotheses, and narratives. For instance, in *The General Theory*, Keynes analyzed the postulates of neoclassical economics inductively. He used analogy to show a logical flaw in that theory, enabling him to demonstrate its insufficiency and make his checkmate again neoclassical economics. Therefore, Keynes created enough room in economics to induce *The General Theory*. This will be presented in Chapter 5, so please keep induction in mind.

Keynes' arguments in favor of induction were so strong that Bertrand Russell, a major philosopher of the 20th Century, praised Keynes in the preface to his 1912 book, *The Problems of Philosophy*. In Russell's words, "I have derived valuable assistance from unpublished writings of G. E. Moore and J. M. Keynes: . . . from the latter as regards probability and induction" (Russel, 1912, p. i). It would be unreasonable to assume that Keynes had given valuable assistance on induction to someone like Bertrand Russell yet had not used it in his own economic work. This book will show that he did use induction in his economics; thereby, it also shows that induction was Keynes' method – or, at least, his main or most used method.

Note

1 If you want to learn more about the developments Keynes made to analogy as a component of induction, see Hesse (1987) and Scazzieri (2021).

References

Carvalho, F. J. C. (2003). 'Características Essenciais do Método de Keynes na Teoria Geral', in Corazza, G. (ed.) *Métodos da Ciência Econômica*. Porto Alegre: UFRGS, pp. 175–188.
Friedman, M. (1953). *Essays in Positive Economics*. Chicago: University of Chicago Press.
Hesse, M. (1987). 'Keynes and the Method of Analogy', *Topoi*, 6(1), pp. 65–74.
Keynes, J. M. (1921). *A Treatise on Probability*. London: Macmillan.
Keynes, J. M. (2013d). *The General Theory of Employment, Interest and Money: The Collected Writings of John Maynard Keynes*, vol. VII. London: Royal Economic Society and Cambridge University Press.
Russell, B. (1912). *The Problems of Philosophy*. New York: Henry Holt and Company.
Scazzieri, R. (2021). 'Patterning Uncertainty: Partial Likeness, Analogy and Likelihood', *Cambridge Journal of Economics*, 45, pp. 1009–1026.
Terra, F. H. B. and Ferrari Filho, F. (2018). 'Reflections on Keynes' Method', *Revista Venezolana de Análisis de Coyuntura*, 24(1), pp. 85–101.

PART II

Flirting With Money

In *The General Theory*, Keynes deeply changed how economic theory understood the economy. However, he did not arrive at *The General Theory* in just one shot. He had two major books before this 1936 book, the 1923 *A Tract on Monetary Reform* and 1930 *A Treatise on Money*. In both books, Keynes flirted with money (in fact, he had teased money earlier, in the 1913 *Indian Currency and Finance;* but we do not present this book because it had no influence on economics).

A Tract on Monetary Reform, which is the topic of Chapter 3, shows us Keynes on the fence. He partly departed from the neoclassical tradition, but he was still partly attached to it. In *A Treatise on Money*, discussed in Chapter 4, Keynes made an even deeper dive into money. In this book, we encounter an economic debate that partially anticipates aspects that Keynes later developed in *The General Theory*. We also find the Wicksellian Keynes, owing to the influence that the Swede economist Knut Wicksell exerted on how Keynes understood the relationship between money and price fluctuations.

Both *A Tract* and *A Treatise* are surely much more than we will go through in this book. We intend to briefly explain how Keynes saw money in his quest to understand and unpack capitalism as the monetary economy of production. The purpose of this book does not leave room for a deep presentation of these two books. But if our presentation of them in the following pages encourages you to go through these works of our protagonist Keynes, we tick our task done. By the way, when we say just *A Treatise* from now on, we refer to *A Treatise on Money* and not to *A Treatise on Probability*.

References

Keynes, J. M. (1913). *Indian Currency and Finance*. London: Macmillan.
Keynes, J. M. (2013a). *A Tract on Monetary Reform: The Collected Writings of John Maynard Keynes*, vol. IV. London: Cambridge University Press.

DOI: 10.4324/9781003287094-5

Keynes, J. M. (2013b). *A Treatise on Money I, the Pure Theory of Money: The Collected Writings of John Maynard Keynes*, vol. V. London: Cambridge University Press.

Keynes, J. M. (2013c). *A Treatise on Money II, the Applied Theory of Money: The Collected Writings of John Maynard Keynes*, vol. VI. London: Cambridge University Press.

Keynes, J. M. (2013d). *The General Theory of Employment, Interest and Money: The Collected Writings of John Maynard Keynes*, vol. VII. London: Royal Economic Society and Cambridge University Press.

3

IN THE LONG RUN WE ARE ALL DEAD

A Tract on the Monetary Reform

The 1923 *A Tract on the Monetary Reform* was Keynes' second book in economics. The topic of the book is inflation, an issue ravaging central and eastern Europe since World War I and occurring on a minor scale in the United States and the United Kingdom. Inflation aroused debates on economic theory and policy. On the one hand, the economic and political orthodoxy of that time advocated the return to the gold standard, with an appreciated exchange rate, as the remedy for inflation. On the other hand, Keynes disagreed with this remedy and the quarrel nurtured *A Tract on Monetary Reform*.

What was Keynes' monetary reform? The main points of it were: (1) central banks should focus on price stability rather than on exchange rate stability. (2) The gold standard should be dismissed and any accumulation of gold as a foreign reserve should aim at easing medium- and long-term fluctuations of the balance of payments. (3) Central banks should not worry too much about short-term fluctuations in the exchange rate. Their concern should preferably be with keeping stable the exchange rate trend, that is, its medium- and long-term values. The target of long-term exchange rate stability is the purchasing power parity of the country's currency. The benefit of such exchange rate long-run stability is that the interest rate of monetary policy would become steadier because central banks would no longer need to vary their interest rate according to short-term fluctuations of the foreign exchange. Short-term fluctuations of the exchange rate in relation to the country's purchasing power parity are acceptable, forasmuch as exists an active policy of the central bank to match both and keep them stable *in the long-term* (already gestating ideas that he would better develop later, in *A Tract* Keynes maidenly spoke about an international coordination to facilitate global exchange rate administration).

Moreover, (4) the stability of the exchange rate should not be set in parity with only one foreign currency, but with a set of external currencies, especially those of the country's greatest trade partners. (5) Keynes also suggested countries to peg

DOI: 10.4324/9781003287094-6

the price of gold to their national currency, but without warranting convertibility, a reaffirmation of his position against the readoption of the classical gold standard. (6) He recommended the creation of a corridor for future prices of gold between which central banks should actively negotiate the metal to maintain its forward value stable. (7) Keynes also suggested for an intimate coordination between central banks and national treasuries. Two reasons explain this. First, he saw both State entities as the key players in determining money supply and, accordingly, the price level. Second, Keynes also pondered the potential impacts of repayments of treasuries' foreign debt on countries' balance of payment. Lastly, (8) his monetary reform proposed withdrawing the limits on the expansion of money supply.

Throughout *A Tract*, Keynes asked for active monetary policy to govern money and build economic stability. Breaking ties with the rigid regimes of the gold standard and fixed exchange rate would provide central banks with flexibility and autonomy to set interest rates at the level required to stabilize domestic factors, such as, in Keynes words, "I regard the stability of prices, credit, and employment as of paramount importance" (2013a, p. 140). In *A Tract*, among these paramount variables, price was in the first position.

How do prices fluctuate? In 1923, Keynes would reply to this question in a somewhat neoclassical fashion. Back then, he still believed that the volume of money in circulation was the cause of price fluctuations, an old idea descending from the quantity theory of money. If the money volume has such importance, what does cause it? The volume of credit banks create is the main determinant of money supply. This is an innovative idea of Keynes in *A Tract*, which hints at the attention he already paid to banks' role in the economy, a topic he will further develop in *A Treatise on Money* and *The General Theory*.

Bank lending depends on how both central banks manage their balance sheet and treasuries administer their fiscal policy. For instance, whenever treasuries spend resources that the central bank provided them with, they increase bank deposits and enable banks to lend more. Thus, more money will come into circulation. Banks are important in delivering to society the supply of money by credit concession, but in the end, in *A Tract*, Keynes believed that bank lending would respond to the behavior of central banks and treasuries.

Even considering central banks' key to money supply, when analyzing the European hyperinflation of the 1920s, Keynes did not blame them for variations in money volume greater than needed to sustain economic activity. He indicted national treasuries. Keynes argued that they continuously sought for a bigger volume of resources. Under the pressure of this request, central banks had no option, but to print money.

It follows that *A Tract's* Chapter 2 is entitled *Public Finances and Changes in the Value of Money*, its first section *Inflation as a Method of Taxation* and the second *Currency Depreciation versus Capital Levy*. In these sections, Keynes discussed how national treasuries could pitch the strategy of financing themselves with central banks printing money but without causing inflation. The strategy would work, Keynes explained, only for as long as people, businesses, and banks did not change their habits of using money in face of central banks' issuance of money to finance treasuries. However, in Keynes' view, central and eastern Europe countries had long surpassed this threshold and inflation deeply troubled them.

To understand the relationship between the quantity of money and prices, Keynes put forth his own version of the quantity theory of money. With a foot on the neoclassical tradition, Keynes started his money theory by assuming that money value rests on its utility as a means of exchange – in his late life, we will see, money becomes much more than this. The volume of money guarded for exchange depends on the purchasing power that individuals and businesses desire to hold. Let us, like Keynes did, name n the volume of money, p the price level, and k the consumption units of individuals and firms (i.e., their habits). Thus, in a simple mathematical parlance,

$$n = kp.$$

This is the traditional form of the quantity theory of money, in which habits (k) change so slowly that they can be assumed constant. Given this constancy of k, there is no reason for p to move other than a change in n. Thus, p moves solely, directly, and proportionally to n. Keynes did not question the validity of this reasoning in the long term. In the short term, however, he deemed the traditional quantity theory of money unreal, which created room for his own quantity theory of money.

Keynes added two new variables to the traditional equation seen previously, the volume of purchasing power that agents deposit at current accounts in banks and cash reserves that banks customarily retain from the deposits they receive. These variables are k' and r. While k' is the consumption units to be acquired using purchasing power held at banks, r is the cash reserves that banks maintain to face their liabilities with clients. Keynes assumed that k depends on agents' wealth and habits, and it determines the volume of purchasing power that agents hold. In turn, r relies on the customary habits of banks. Keynes' quantity theory of money is as follows:

$$n = p(k + rk').$$

Different from wealth, whose change only happens slowly, Keynes assumed that habits (i.e., k, k', and r) can switch more easily (whereas in the traditional quantity theory of money, they were constant). These moveable habits, whether of individuals, businesses, or banks, take away the sole, direct, and proportional determinacy of n on p. Changing habits can offset the impacts of greater n on p, for example, as it is the case if more money enters the economy and people prefer to hoard it. Nevertheless, habits can also increase the impacts of bigger n on p. Keynes illustrated this case by bringing expectations into the scene.

If governments, like those of central and eastern Europe in the 1920s, use inflationary taxation and n increases hourly, agents might start expecting more future rounds of money issuing. Trying to protect their income and wealth, businesspeople with market power to make their prices modify their habits and readjust their prices upward before a new round of money printing occurs. Then, workers begin fighting for bigger salaries and rentiers start charging higher interest rates to lend their savings. This example of the 1920s is today known as the distributive conflict, a theme on the spotlight of economics in the 21st century. Inflation and deflation affect income and wealth distribution as well as production. Keynes thoroughly examined these phenomena in Chapter 1 of *A Tract* to base one of the ways through which n does not cause p directly and proportionally. The economic cycle can also modify habits. For instance, some fear of the future can imply hoards great enough to cause a depression and, consequently, deflation. In other direction, expectations of booms can stimulate a faster use of money and, in turn, more credit concession, culminating in both inflation and the necessity of more money in circulation.

Habits can change simply because agents, economic organization, and society change over time. Every time habits k, k', and r change, money supply n no longer steers prices p directly and proportionally. These habits shift constantly and imply short-term changes in economic conditions. Therefore, Keynes' quantity theory of money brought about bad and good news. The bad news is that habits drift; they change unprecedently and without prior notice and, thereby, prices float too. Notwithstanding the bad news, there is the good news: if the variables defining the price level p are known, that is, n, k, k', and r, central banks can actively conduct monetary policy to stabilize p. How should central banks act?

On the one hand, money supply n and banks' cash reserves r can and should be under the direct control of central banks. Hence, governments must not use money supply n to fuel their resources (they must not resort to inflationary taxation); moreover, r must not be left to an uncoordinated banking market setting. Central banks need to secure themselves the power to define it. On the other hand, k and k' are uncontrollable, but they are influenceable. The aim of central banks' monetary policy is to influence k and k' to either avoid or soften their destabilizing impact on p.

To do so, central banks usually manage their base interest rates, which is the rate by which they do monetary policy (because of that it is also called policy rate). By managing their base interest rate, central banks try to influence k and k'. A greater rate would reduce expenditure habits, while a lower one would foster them. If the sole administration of the base rate does not reach the awaited outcome, central banks must also manage n and r to counterbalance the swings of k and k' – thus, the importance of central banks defining banks' cash reserve r and money supply n. For, money supply should be neither under inflationary taxation nor attached to the gold standard. Both remove central banks' control over n and deliver it to other agents, the former to treasuries, and the latter to the uncontrollable gold flows throughout the world.

To conclude, *A Tract on Monetary Reform* had an ambiguous Keynes. He was still somewhat neoclassical so long as he believed that (1) prices were the key economic variable – though Keynes innovated for considering unemployment and credit so important as to be kept under the surveillance of economic authorities.

(2) Governments were not the only source of inflation but remained as its main cause. (3) Money's main utility was to be a medium of exchange. Lastly, (4) Keynes believed that the quantity theory of money was valid in the long term. These are Keynes' abiding neoclassical characteristics in 1923.

On the fence, Keynes was looking for a direction to take off from the partially neoclassical seat he was on. He was starting to fly toward building his own tradition. This trip would endure for more than a decade, until 1936. Still, the fence he was on in *A Tract* was quite an important departure gate. The book is plenty of Keynes' non-neoclassical features such as his views on banks, his rejection of the gold standard, his demands for a managed orchestration of the international monetary system, his recognition of the importance of variables other than prices, his unbalanced and non-self-regulating quantity theory of money, and the consequent necessity of an active State economic coordination and intervention. All these features gained size and importance on the road to his later works.

Keynes' vivid claim for an active economic policy in *A Tract* rendered his most famous phrase ever. It is so brilliant and summarizes so well the debate done hitherto that we finish this chapter fully quoting it,

> Now "in the long run" this is probably true. If, after the American Civil War, the American Dollar had been stabilized and defined by law at 10 per cent below its present value, it would be safe to assume that n and p would be just 10 percent greater than they actually are and that the present values of k, r, and k' would be entirely unaffected. But this *long run* is a misleading guide to current affairs. *In the long run* we are all dead. Economists set themselves too easy, too useless a task if in tempestuous seasons they can only tell us that when the storm is long past the ocean is flat again.
>
> *(2013a, p. 65, marks in the original)*

References

Keynes, J. M. (2013a). *A Tract on Monetary Reform: The Collected Writings of John Maynard Keynes*, vol. IV. London: Cambridge University Press.

Keynes, J. M. (2013b). *A Treatise on Money I, the Pure Theory of Money: The Collected Writings of John Maynard Keynes*, vol. V. London: Cambridge University Press.

Keynes, J. M. (2013c). *A Treatise on Money II, the Applied Theory of Money: The Collected Writings of John Maynard Keynes*, vol. VI. London: Cambridge University Press.

Keynes, J. M. (2013d). *The General Theory of Employment, Interest and Money: The Collected Writings of John Maynard Keynes*, vol. VII. London: Royal Economic Society and Cambridge University Press.

4

THE WICKSELLIAN KEYNES

A Treatise on Money

The first drafts of *A Treatise on Money* appeared in 1924, a year after the *Tract* was published. With some discontinuities in writing *A Treatise*, Keynes took more than half a decade to finish the book. It was finally published in 1930, with a three-year delay in relation to the first agreed date of publication, 1927. Such a lag resulted in a massive work. *A Treatise* has two volumes, *The Pure Theory of Money* and *The Applied Theory of Money*. Together, both volumes count more than 600 pages.

Keynes' puzzle in *A Treatise* figured out the relationship between money and price dynamics. This, in turn, required the understanding of the economic and credit cycles as well as the inter-relations among industry and finance. To assemble the puzzle, Keynes decided to deeply explain all its pieces. In the end, this strategy made him go thoroughly through a lot of elements, culminating in a book that is neither easy to read nor, like many other things related to Keynes, free of controversies. The debates about the book were many. They included a review from Friedrich Hayek to which Keynes replied that

> Hayek has not read my book with that measure of 'good will' which an author is entitled to expect of a reader. Until he can do so, he will not see what I mean or know whether I am right. He evidently has a passion which leads him to pick on me, but I am left wondering what this passion is.
>
> *(Keynes, 1973, p. 243, marks in the original)*

In *A Treatise*, Keynes was focusing on the causal elements that drive prices from one equilibrium to another, either up (inflation) or down (deflation). Equilibrium here is not only a word choice. It has an important theoretical meaning, namely, a position of the economic system at which prices are stable. The departure from and the arrival at this point depend on an idea that was first developed by Knut Wicksell, a Swedish economist a bit older than Keynes. Recognizing the pertinence of

DOI: 10.4324/9781003287094-7

Wicksell's theory, Keynes borrowed a key aspect from it and made this aspect the piece to complete the puzzle in *A Treatise*. What is this Keynes' Wicksellian piece? Curiosity is a good attention catcher; so, the answer to this question will come later, when we get close to finishing the puzzle of *A Treatise on Money*.

The Key Variables

Keynes wrote *A Treatise* to investigate the relationship between money and price dynamics. To explain that relationship, Keynes had to subsidiarily explore other themes, like economic and credit cycles, industry, and finance. To simplify the explanation of the main relationships between all these elements, we remind you that an economy has three key aggregates, demand, product (supply), and income. Demand is the act of expending in exchange for something. For example, entrepreneurs buying machines and equipment to produce other goods and services are investing; thus, investment is a component of demand. People spend to consume goods and services that satisfy their needs. Consumption is another component of demand.

If entrepreneurs and consumers are demanding, they are procuring for goods and services, that is, products. Suppose you are asked: what are the main economic variables that you know? It is highly likely that GDP, inflation, money, shares, unemployment, and, nowadays, bitcoin and crypto-assets will appear in your replies. Let us take GDP. It means gross domestic product, where gross and domestic are qualifying the noun, product. Product, a key economic concept, means everything produced in an economy at a certain time. It is the supply of the country, the things which are produced to be sold domestically and externally.

Whenever entrepreneurs invest, they demand machines and equipment to form a productive process. Thereby, they expand the country's capacity to supply goods and services. Workers are hired in the productive process and employment goes up. Also, investment also demands from suppliers of goods specially related to production, called capital goods or capital assets. Thus, a part of entrepreneurs' expenditures makes the income of other entrepreneurs who sell capital goods. Another part of entrepreneurs' expenditures is paid to workers and is their income. When putting up a productive process, all that entrepreneurs wish is that the investment they made and that became income to others return to them as these other people demand the supply they produced. Let the reader bear that in mind.

Let us resume the presentation of *A Treatise*. To explain how money and price dynamics are related, Keynes set four actors on the stage, workers, entrepreneurs, banks, and financial investors. Entrepreneurs and workers are such as described earlier. Banks collect deposits from the people, in the form of cash deposits (also called demand deposits, checking, or current accounts), which are money as means of exchange, and saving deposits (or time deposits). The latter are financial investments made through banks. In turn, financial investors are those who make financial investments. They lend their money to others or buy companies' shares in stock markets. In the 1930s, by the time of *A Treatise*, financial investment was mostly made through banks. Nowadays, things are different, but banks are still the most important financial actor, so let us take them as the financial agent *per excellence*, like Keynes did.

Sorry for interrupting the exposition of *A Treatise* again, but explanations are crucial to clearness: what are financial investment and financial investors? Financial investment is the purchase of financial assets, such as securities, shares, public bills and bonds, bitcoins, and so on. Financial assets are neither immediately nor necessarily linked to production. Although finance and production are extremely connected, they are not the same thing. Of course, financial assets extensively furnish money to fund productive investment plans, but not always. For instance, apart from an initial public offer (IPO) and follow-ons, the acquisition of shares does not gather resources from their issuing companies (these just receive capital when they make IPO and follow-on (the issuance of new equities)).

Let the reader bear in mind throughout the rest of this book: entrepreneurs make productive investments. They purchase capital goods to produce goods and services, whereas financial investors do not make an immediate productive investment. Financial investment can reach productive investment, but always indirectly, by the former funding the latter. Still, the decision to buy a financial asset, even if the financial investor knows that it will finance a productive investment, is not a decision equal to making a productive investment. Financial investors know this. They buy financial assets to precisely avoid the complexities and risks of engaging in productive processes. From now on, when we say investment without any qualification, we mean productive investment.

We now go back to banks in *A Treatise*. Banks' objective is not really capturing deposits. These serve to make banks assembly resources to lend. Banks lend the deposits they receive; this is how they try to profit. Bank lending finances consumers, businesses, governments, and even some riskier financial investors, who borrow money to buy other financial assets and speculate with them. As the bank gets familiarized with how its clients manage their deposits, it increases its loans. The bank will lend more than a unity of money for each unity of money it receives. Thus, as banks lend, they multiply the volume of money in circulation in the economy. Moreover, banks also set the bank interest rate. This rate is the average of what banks charge on their short-term loans and what they pay on the saving deposits through which they capture resources.

Banks have such great control of the quantity of credit and the bank rate in the economy that Keynes deemed them responsible for the credit cycle. If banks outlook a good economic future, they lend and foster expenditure, especially investment plans. Lower interest rates accompany this greater credit supply. If banks change their mind, they reduce credit and increase their bank interest rate, accordingly, the economy slumps.

So far, several elements have been set into motion, but only a few of their dynamics were enlisted. It is time to leave the picture and start watching the movie scripted in *A Treatise* about the relationship between money and price dynamics. The stability of prices happens, Keynes argued, if there is an equivalence between the components of aggregate demand and income in relation to the aggregate supply of the economy. Let us assume the simplest economic scenario, with only workers and entrepreneurs. Demand is split into, on the one side, workers' and entrepreneurs' consumption and, on the other side, investment entrepreneurs make. The aggregate income that workers and entrepreneurs receive, as wages and profits, respectively, is allocated to consumption and savings.

But savings are more than just a non-consumed part of income. If seen from the country's supply capacity, savings create, say, "room" in the productive process. This "production space" will be used for producing goods other than those for consumption. Investment, the other component of demand, occupies this available productive capacity. An extreme example illustrates this idea. Remember that the economy's aggregate supply partly produces consumption goods and, partly, capital goods. If consumption is so big that the production of consumption goods engrosses the whole supply capacity, investment would not occur. There would be no spare capacity to supply capital goods to entrepreneurs.

Price Dynamics

The dynamics of prices relies on the balance between investment and savings, and so does economic stability. The logic is as follows: investment greater than savings makes demand greater than supply. Demand bigger than supply assures windfall profits to entrepreneurs. This positive scenario pushes entrepreneurs to increase investment, add workers to their production, and pay greater salaries. However, within this positive economic activity, prices increase too; thus, inflation emerges when investment is bigger than savings. The opposite scenario happens if savings are larger than investment. In this case, demand is smaller than supply and entrepreneurs have losses. Their businesses thus fail, and unemployment raises and pushes wages down. Accordingly, prices decrease and the economy becomes deflationary. Prices will only grow stable again when investment and savings reach a new balance at a new equilibrium point.

What are the determinants of investment and savings? The determinants of investment are two: first, anticipated future returns that entrepreneurs outlook in their business plan (in passing, what Keynes will call expectations in *The General Theory* had appeared in *A Treatise* as anticipation). Second, interest rates, whose determinacy over investment is twofold. Interest rates are yields of financial assets and entrepreneurs can buy these assets if they want, so they are an alternative investment in relation to capital assets. Moreover, interest rates are also an investment effective cost, charged to entrepreneurs when they borrow funds to finance their business plans.

Entrepreneurs start businesses as they desire to increase their wealth by investing in capital goods. As the decision-making process of Chapter 1 described, a current decision to invest considers future returns that entrepreneurs expect from purchasing a capital asset. Still, expected gains are just mental anticipations. The accuracy of these forecasts only time will tell. However, entrepreneurs can otherwise simply look at the interest rates that financial assets pay (including the rates that banks pay on saving deposits) and calculate the capitalization of their wealth's present value to some future value. Observe that investing is always an act of comparing alternative rates of return. Incidentally, economics uses the technical term opportunity cost to refer to the comparison of different returns. This cost is not necessarily a loss. It can be a gain, however, smaller than that yielded by other assets that the buyer could have bought.

Savings, on the other side, are determined by income. People cannot save without accessing a regular flux of income. Nevertheless, the degree to which individuals save depends on the interest rate, which is the incentive for saving. However, it is not only the actual interest rate that matters for savings. The expected future path of interest rate also has a key role in determining what individuals will do with their savings. Investors' expectations about the variation of interest rates define whether they buy a certain asset, another, or simply hoard their money. For instance, if banks pay an increasing interest rate on saving deposits, savings are stimulated. Otherwise, decreasing interest rates are keen to encourage productive investment. To sum up, income determines the existence of savings. Nevertheless, the form in which savings are maintained, such as money, saving deposits, and shares, depends on agents' expectations about interest rate variations while they bear the asset.

Do you remember that the balance or imbalance between investment and savings defines price dynamics? The interest rate is a key variable in determining the balance between investment and savings. Thus, what is the interest rate? This is the final piece closing the logic of *A Treatise*. We now meet the Wicksellian Keynes.

The Wicksellian Keynes

Two reasons led Keynes to borrow Knut Wicksell's ideas. The first, and foremost, is that Keynes recognized that Wicksell was the first economist to explain that price changes because investment and savings can move in an unbalanced way, which pulls the economy into expansive or depressive cycles. Second, Keynes also took Wicksell's concept of the natural interest rate. At this natural rate, there is an equilibrium between investment and savings; consequently, demand and supply also become also balanced, and, finally, prices get stable. Hence, at the natural rate, the whole system settles.

The natural rate of interest is a kind of neutral interest rate in the sense that it does not stimulate savers to change the amount of their savings and entrepreneurs to alter their investment. It is a kind of benchmark rate that levels investment and savings to put the economy in a resting position. In practical terms, it can be taken as the minimum interest rate in which each person agrees to invest money instead of leaving it under the mattress. In aggregate, each person's natural interest rate forms the economy's natural interest rate.

Another important concept is the market interest rate. It is the interest rate that really prevails in the financial markets. The market rate is, in fact, an average interest rate emerging from two other interest rates – a portrayal of what is today known as the yield curve or the interest rate term structure. The first rate forming the market rate is the bank rate, which is the average rate that banks charge to capture and lend money for a short period. The other rate is the long-term interest rate paid by bonds. Unbalances between the market rate and the natural rate wiggle the delicate grip between investment and savings; therefore, economic cycles occur and disturb prices, dynamizing them from one equilibrium to another.

Let us delve deeper into how Keynes explained the determination of the market interest rate. Economies have two major sides, the financial and real sectors. Banks and financial investors belong to the former sector. In this sector, borrowers and lenders of money meet, and liquid assets are negotiated. (Liquidity is a concept that will appear repeatedly in this book. In short, it means how quickly, easily, and cheaply an asset can be converted into money; the faster the asset can become money, the more liquid it is.) Today, this sector is simply called the financial system or financial markets. In *A Treatise*, Keynes called it financial circulation. The real sector is where the production and distribution of goods and services take place. Investment and consumption also occur in the real sector, also known as the real economy. Keynes called this sector industrial circulation.

The financial circulation of money grants credit to the industrial circulation, especially to finance investment plans, which mobilize large sums of resources. However, the volume of money circulating in the financial system can change abruptly, owing to banks' and financial investors' changing expectations about variations in the interest rates on financial assets. To characterize investors' mentality in financial circulation, Keynes borrowed two financial jargons. One mentality outlooks loss and opts to entrench savings either in very conservative assets or even far away from financial markets. Individuals in this spectrum are the pessimistic bear agents. On the other hand, bull agents are those with a heady belief that markets will rise. They expect good payoffs and buy assets.

Bears demand money to store it as a reserve of wealth. Bulls supply money in exchange for short- and long-term financial assets. Bears and bulls' disputes of expectations define the volume of money in the financial circulation and, consequently, the market interest rate. If bear hordes put the market in a bear territory, the lesser supply of money rises market interest rates and makes them greater than the natural interest rate. Therefore, savings increase and investment decreases, which is equal to demand falling short of supply. If this plight lasts, it creates loss and brings employment, and thus wages, down. In the end, the economy slumps and deflation reigns. The opposite happens in a bull market. In this case, the larger supply of money lowers the market interest rate below the natural interest rate. Investment becomes greater than savings then. The economic boom has higher employment, wages, and prices.

Banks are essential players in financial circulation. They set the bank rate, which is the interest rate of short-term financial assets. Hence, banks command a big part of the market interest rate. Consequently, they have a strong power in balancing the natural and market interest rates. The source of banks' power is their ability to control credit, which is, in fact, a control over money supply. With this power, banks can either offset a bear market or ignite an economic boom. To offset a bear market, they only need to buy the financial assets that bear investors are selling on a large scale and thus supply the market with money, counterbalancing the tendency for the market interest rate to rise. To ignite an economic boom, banks validate bulls' positive prospects and lend them credit.

Banks have such a command over resources in the economy that they can dictate credit cycles. Thus, they largely influence the economic cycle and price dynamics. Banks' power in *A Treatise* is so big that Keynes matched theirs and central banks' power for money management. Together, banks and central banks set money supply and the bank rate. Notwithstanding the power of banks, Keynes requested an active monetary management by central banks in *A Treatise*. If central banks want to influence banks and, in turn, the economy, they should manage the bank rate by attempting to change the level of the market interest rate in relation to the natural interest rate's level. Central banks are also important in open economies. They are responsible for taking care of the country's external transactions. Whatever the intention of central banks though, they need the cooperation of banks.

Notice that interest rates are at the center of price dynamics. The interest rate connects money to prices by means of its determinacy on the balance between investment and savings. Price instability and economic cycles happen because of discrepancies between the natural interest rate and market interest rate. Keynes offered an original explanation for the setting of the market interest rate. But he borrowed the concept of the natural interest rate, which was the closing piece of the monetary theory he advanced in *A Treatise*, from Knut Wicksell. In light of that, we met the Wicksellian Keynes.

A Treatise was a big step that Keynes made on the road to understanding money and its relationship with prices. In *A Tract*, he continued to focus on how money and price dynamics associate, but in *A Treatise,* Keynes offered a rather more complex monetary theory. Some of *A Treatise's* variables and understandings will reappear in *The General Theory*. Nevertheless, unlike *A Treatise* (as well as *A Tract*), in *The General Theory,* price dynamics no longer is the usual outcome of monetary issues. As a matter of fact, price dynamics no longer is a primary topic in *The General Theory*.

Compared to *A Tract*, in *A Treatise,* Keynes deeper explained the relevance of banks to the monetary, financial, and economic systems. He extensively clarified the endogenous nature of money. Central banks are not the only supplier of money to the economy; in economic parlance, money is not exogenous. Central banks do exogenously issue money, but banks endogenously supply money whenever they grant credit. Banks create money as the public demand credit to consume and invest. This demand of consumers and entrepreneurs comes from within the economy and banks respond to the procurement for loans from within the economy as well, thus, the endogeneity of money.

In *A Treatise*, inflation is not a strictly monetary phenomenon, nor only, or mainly, governments cause it. Money is related to inflation through a complex link that involves rates of interest, bull and bear financial investors, banks, finance, industry, investment, savings, supply, demand, wages, profits, loss, expectations, and so on. Moreover, there is the Wicksellian component: Knut Wicksell's natural interest rate determines the balance between investment and savings in Keynes' *A Treatise*. Keynes recognized Wicksell's originality and borrowed from him the logic to close the gap between money, interest rates, and price dynamics.

Moreover, the relationship between money and prices made Keynes argue that the real economy and the financial sector are inseparable. The financial system is not neutral to the real sector. The former affects the dynamics of the latter since the way investors deal with money changes the market interest rate which either hampers or stimulates economic activity. Money is thus no longer neutral to the economy, neither in the short term nor in the long term. The quantity money theory is gone in *A Treatise,* and the relationship between money and prices is no more an assumption in an algebraic identity. It now has a logical content, which Wicksell helped Keynes understand.

There remain two final elements of *A Treatise*. First, expectation already matters in this book, and its role only grows in *The General Theory*. Second, Keynes requested monetary management in *A Treatise*, as he did in *A Tract*. He favored a managed money, a fiduciary money backed by a central authority, without any ballast whatsoever. In view of that, both volumes of *A Treatise* say much on central banks' monetary policy. Moreover, the international orchestration Keynes had advanced in *A Tract* reappeared in *A Treatise*, but now he even proposed a multilateral institution and a supranational money (the supranational bank money), an embryo of his post-World War II International Clearing Union proposal.

A Treatise is a book in which Keynes' ideas were in flux. The sketches of the place he wanted to arrive were pretty much in his mind. However, he did not enjoy his first attempt to put the sketches together in *A Treatise*. But with *The General Theory,* his feeling will be different; Keynes will fulfill his theoretical desires. The sketches of *A Treatise* became a final draw in *The General Theory* whose picture founded a school of economics carrying from 1936 onward the surname of the painter, Keynesian.

References

Keynes, J. M. (1973). *The General Theory and After: Part I Preparation. The Collected Writings of John Maynard Keynes*, vol. XIII. London: Royal Economic Society and Macmillan Press.

Keynes, J. M. (2013a). *A Tract on Monetary Reform: The Collected Writings of John Maynard Keynes*, vol. IV. London: Cambridge University Press.

Keynes, J. M. (2013b). *A Treatise on Money I, the Pure Theory of Money: The Collected Writings of John Maynard Keynes*, vol. V. London: Cambridge University Press.

Keynes, J. M. (2013c). *A Treatise on Money II, the Applied Theory of Money: The Collected Writings of John Maynard Keynes*, vol. VI. London: Cambridge University Press.

Keynes, J. M. (2013d). *The General Theory of Employment, Interest and Money: The Collected Writings of John Maynard Keynes*, vol. VII. London: Royal Economic Society and Cambridge University Press.

PART III

Keynes' Checkmate

The General Theory of Employment,
Interest and Money

In prefaces to foreign editions of *A Treatise*, in responses to reviewers and readers of this book, in discussions with his fellow economists in Cambridge, and in the preface to *The General Theory*, Keynes recognized that *A Treatise on Money* was a result of buoyant ideas, on the creative road that arrived at *The General Theory of Employment, Interest and Money*. Keynes began writing his new book a few months after the publication of *A Treatise* in October 1930. His discomfort with this book had a reason that is similar to his annoyance with the neoclassical tradition: in both, a theory of production was absent. *The General Theory* brings Keynes' monetary theory of production, which seals his view of the economy as a monetary economy of production. Price fluctuations no longer are Keynes' main concern. His business is now unemployment, which is a consequence of production that, in turn, is demand-led.

The raison d'être of capitalism is the accumulation of wealth and production is the means to this goal. To start a productive process and try to accumulate wealth, entrepreneurs must invest their wealth. Thus, the first step of investment is for businesspeople to spend money to buy capital assets, equipment, raw materials, and, especially, employ workers. When all these are set, production kickoffs. Entrepreneurs' intention is that more money than they invested comes into their pockets, pays off their initial costs, and provides them profits that augment their wealth accumulation.

However, it is quite normal that entrepreneurs, depending on their expectations, decide to either enshrine money or make financial investments, which exchange money for liquid financial assets, quickly convertible back into money if necessary. These two decisions do not start productive processes though. Consequently, they do not add workers to the list of employed people. But why should entrepreneurs hold money? Because money is a special asset in the economy. It securely stores wealth over time in the most liquid manner. Therefore, Keynes' theory of

DOI: 10.4324/9781003287094-8

production sees capitalism as a monetary economy of production in which money plays a special role in determining production and, in turn, the employment level. To persuade the world that his theory was, first, right, and second, the one to be followed, Keynes needed to overhaul neoclassical economics' theoretical juggernaut. He did so in *The General Theory*. Then, Keynesian economics was born.

This part explains *The General Theory of Employment, Interest and Money*, Keynes' magnum opus. Chapter 5 describes his checkmate on neoclassical economics. He havocked this theory by showing logical and factual flaws in how it interpreted the functioning of the labor market. If the neoclassical theory is gone, Keynes made room for his own theory. In it, demand is the dynamic economic factor, as Chapter 6 explains. If demand hefts the economy, Chapters 7 and 8 explain its components, consumption, and investment, respectively. We already know that in monetary economies of production, the importance of money is sheer. Risking spoiling the plot, but only intending to catch your attention, we reveal that the connection between money and demand happens through the interest rate, because it is one of the determinants of investment. Hence, having discussed investment in Chapter 8, Chapter 9 focuses on money and explains the liquidity preference theory and its outcome, the interest rate. Chapter 10 discloses why money is special: what are its idiosyncrasies? To sum up, Chapter 11 summarizes the economic dynamics as stated by Keynes in *The General Theory*. Finally, Chapter 12 goes through further elements of *The General Theory*, such as prices, wage variation, employment function, trade cycles, and the social philosophy Keynes proposed in the book.

References

Keynes, J. M. (2013b). *A Treatise on Money I, the Pure Theory of Money: The Collected Writings of John Maynard Keynes*, vol. V. London: Cambridge University Press.

Keynes, J. M. (2013c). *A Treatise on Money II, the Applied Theory of Money: The Collected Writings of John Maynard Keynes*, vol. VI. London: Cambridge University Press.

Keynes, J. M. (2013d). *The General Theory of Employment, Interest and Money: The Collected Writings of John Maynard Keynes*, vol. VII. London: Royal Economic Society and Cambridge University Press.

5

CHECKMATING THE NEOCLASSICAL THEORY

The Name *The General Theory*

The first chapter of *The General Theory* consists of only one paragraph and one footnote, occupying only one page. In this brief chapter, Keynes clarified what he named classical economics. He borrowed the term from Karl Marx, to whom classical economists were those who founded economics, starting with Adam Smith and going until David Ricardo. However, Keynes went further than Marx. He included in classical economics neoclassical economists, who are those economists who followed the tradition of David Ricardo. Therefore, Keynes' definition of classical economics encompassed his contemporaries at Cambridge, like Alfred Marshall (Keynes' former mentor and professor) and Arthur Cecil Pigou.

The first chapter of *The General Theory* also explained the book's title, with a special emphasis on *general*. Keynes argued that classical and neoclassical economics could only explain the economy in one singular and very rare case: full employment. But full employment is the exception rather than the rule: far more prevalent in economic history are various conditions of unemployment. Hence, if classical and neoclassical economics could only explain economic behavior in the special full employment case, they were a particular, not a general theory; they were only valid in the singular case of full employment.

If, as we have said, abundant unemployment is the general historic condition of economies, a *general* economic theory needs to address and explain the causes of unemployment. Keynes' *The General Theory* explained the causes of unemployment, so he called his theory *general* because it dealt with the general case of the economic system over time.

However, in the preface to the French edition of *The General Theory*, Keynes also stated that his *General Theory* was general because it focused on analyzing the economy in aggregate. He was founding macroeconomics, which changed the

DOI: 10.4324/9781003287094-9

focus of the economic analysis from individuals and firms, as it is the case in micro-economics, to the whole: to the aggregate demand, aggregate supply, aggregate income, and so on.

Keynes issued two warnings regarding the macroeconomic analysis. His first was that the whole is not simply the sum of its parts. His second argued that the analysis of a variable in aggregate is not equivalent to the microeconomic examination of this variable if it is taken in isolation. Keynes' thrift paradox exemplifies his warnings. A person who saves enriches herself. But if all individuals save, sales diminish and entrepreneurs suffer losses. Businesses then close, production declines and causes unemployment. In the end, society is impoverished. The result for the individual does not hold for the aggregate. Therefore, Keynes wrote a *general theory* to examine the economy in aggregate (and with the presence of unemployment).

Keynes Lectures on Neoclassical Economics

Before we continue, let us clarify that from now on, when we refer to neoclassical economics, we refer to the same theories that Keynes called classical economics in *The General Theory*. As stated previously, in his definition of classical economics, Keynes merged two traditions: (1) the classical one, which started with Adam Smith and to which David Ricardo gave the final contours, and (2) the neoclassical perspective that followed David Ricardo. Keynes' definition thus centered on David Ricardo. Keynes matched classical economics with the Ricardian tradition because he was writing against the entire lineage of Ricardian economics. Although it considers them closely related, the mainstream history of economic thought does not see classical and neoclassical economics as one. But to make your life easier, from now on, this book will only use the term neoclassical, which was the theory contemporary with Keynes. But do not forget that he, himself, called it classical economics.

We are about to delve into *The General Theory's* second chapter, which we must warn you entails an inescapable theoretical dive into Keynes' reading of neoclassical economics. We will digest the debate, lest you get bothered and confused while reading it. In Chapter 2 of *The General Theory*, Keynes lectured on neoclassical economics' labor market theory. His argument primarily challenged Arthur Pigou, especially discussing the latter's book *Theory of Unemployment*. Pigou's book encompassed the evolution of the classical and neoclassical theories of unemployment, and so Keynes took it as a presentation of the state-of-arts on the matter.

Keynes synthesized the neoclassical perspective on the labor market in two postulates: (1) the wage is equal to the marginal product of the labor and (2) the utility of the wage when a given volume of labor is employed is equal to the marginal disutility of that amount of employment.

To understand the first postulate, let us assume, as Keynes did, that two agents compound the economy: workers and businesspeople. Thus, the aggregate income of the economy divides into wages and profits. The first postulate means that, given the economy's aggregate product, the slice of it that flows to laborers as their wages is their share of the GDP. Therefore, the higher the wage share of a given product, the lower the profit share.

In neoclassical theory, postulate (1) is the businesspeople's demand for workers. It states that entrepreneurs hire workers in an inverse relation to wages in the sense that a smaller profit share of the GDP reduces the willingness of entrepreneurs to hire workers. While higher salaries are greater income for workers, they are also higher cost – and a reducer of profits – to entrepreneurs. At each salary, there will be a certain level of entrepreneurial demand for workers. The smaller the salaries, the greater will be employers' demand for laborers.

Postulate (2) discusses the disutility of employment, which means that working is a cost for the workforce. It is an unpleasant activity that workers dislike. They only stand for it if wages furnish them utility enough to pay off the disutility cost of having a job. Wages are the benefit of working because they enable the buying of goods and services, which are the source of the utility that satisfies workers. Thus, the benefit that comes from the pleasure of spending wages to consume products must compensate for the disutility cost of working.

Disutility (cost) and utility (benefit) must balance, and both are priced in accordance with wages. Smaller wages reduce the purchasing of goods and services, meaning that workers experience lower utility and a cheaper cost of being idle as it does not afford the unpleasantness of executing a task. Higher salaries work contrariwise. They offer high utility in terms of purchasing power and elevate the cost of doing nothing. Hence, postulate (2) explains the supply of workers in the labor market. They look at the salary prevalent in the market and decide whether it balances the unpleasantness of working. If it renders sufficient utility to offset the annoyance of working, workers voluntarily supply their labor. But if it is thought not to, workers voluntarily remain unemployed.

Notice that wages define both entrepreneurs' demand for workers and workers' eagerness to supply work. Nevertheless, it is not the nominal wage, the number written in the paystub, that matters. What counts in neoclassical economics is the real wage, the actual amount of goods and services that the salary appearing in the paycheck can buy. In neoclassical theory, real wages determine the demand for, and the supply of, laborers. Whenever the entrepreneur wonders whether to employ workers or not, and workers voluntarily decide to either work or not, they both move, respectively, the labor market's demand and supply forces.

These forces balance at a certain real wage level that in turn balances the market. Once it is in equilibrium, the labor market also sets the equilibrium of the other two great markets in the economy, namely, the goods and financial markets. How does this happen? In neoclassical theory, these equilibria depend on the second postulate because it determines the voluntary supply of labor, according to a certain real wage, in the labor market.

Say's law connects the labor supply and the goods market balance. This law says that supply creates its own demand. The law's logic operates as follows: when workers work, they necessarily produce goods and services; thus, they supply the products of the economy. But remember that workers work to receive their salary to demand goods and services to satisfy their utility. Therefore, laborers supply their work, and so they produce the supply of the economy in exchange for which they receive wages and demand products to satisfy their utility. Supply creates its own demand.

Notice that all productive processes start with the disposition of laborers to work. In economic jargon, this is supply-side economics, in which the driving force of economic activity is laborers' supply of their work. So far, postulate (2) has explained two crucial elements of neoclassical economics, but there is more to come. Observe that it holds a key position in the structure of neoclassical reasoning.

The equilibrium of financial markets – neoclassical economists call them the loanable funds market – emerges from postulate (2) as well. If all that workers want when they supply their labor are goods and services to secure the satisfaction of their utility, do they exclusively consume and never save? Workers do save, but only in exchange for some extra future gain via interest payments. These payments, in turn, permit them to greater future consumption. Workers carry their savings to the loanable funds market and lend them to people willing to invest but who do not have enough funds.

The supply of savings and the demand for investment are, respectively, the supply and demand for loanable funds. The price of these funds is the interest rate, and it equilibrates the financial market. If the interest rate goes up, it means that the demand for funds to back investment plans is increasing faster than the supply of savings. Workers look at this and see the chance of swapping consumption today for greater future consumption. The most attractive aspect of this is that workers need not to work harder to have bigger future consumption. Other people will do the job and pay lenders a reward. Hence, the logic of postulate (2), that laborers work to gain something that compensates for the disutility of laboring, is maintained.

There are two further aspects of neoclassical economics worth exploring. First, the interest rate is the parsimony prize or the premium for waiting. Parsimonious, thrifty workers do not consume their whole income; they prefer to save some part of their rent. Although they opt to fulfill their utility in the future, they will do so on a bigger scale, increased by gains they earned due to their ability to wait. Their present frugality is rewarded with future abundance, and the interest rate is the value of that reward.

Second, savings precede investment, and the latter cannot occur without the former. When society saves, its non-consumption creates a productive space in the supply capacity of the economy. The industry of capital assets uses this space to produce more goods for investment, like machines and equipment. It is common to hear economists and politicians say that a country cannot grow without savings. Now you know where this saying comes from.

We said a lot about the theoretical outcomes of postulate (2) hitherto. Still, this postulate has three more implications worth understanding. First, neoclassical economics sees money as neutral, affecting nothing in the economy: it is incapable of changing employment, GDP, productivity, or any other variable of the real economy. If laborers only work to demand goods and services, they see no reason to hoard money. Even when workers save in exchange for an interest rate that provides them with greater future consumption, they do not hold their savings in cash. They lend their savings to fund other people's investment. Thus, no money is put under the mattress. Hoarding money is senseless in neoclassical economics. Money has no function other than as a means of exchange, a thing to facilitate transactions.

Second, the neoclassical quantity money theory says that prices move only and evenly in relation to money supply (as Chapter 3 discussed). Postulate (2) explains this. As the supply of workers sets both the supply of products and the demand for them, all the possible transactions in the economy become defined. Following suit, as hoarding money makes no sense and workers only work to demand, the velocity of money circulation (which is how fast a coin or bank note passes from hand to hand) is established too. All is unchangeably set because full employment was set in the labor market when laborers supplied their labor for some real wage. Supply and demand are thus defined and, as a result, they establish the whole set of transactions the economy will have and the velocity at which money will circulate to settle these transactions. All in all, no variable is left to define prices except the supply of money. Whenever money supply varies, prices change accordingly.

Moreover, as the voluntary supply of labor defines everything, including firms' supply and the number of economic transactions, it should not be expected that private forces cause changes in money supply. If it is not privately driven, money supply can only alter because of government decisions. However, money is neutral and if governments issue it to propel the economy, only one outcome is possible: inflation. Laborers have already decided the entirety of supply capacity, and there are no production factors available to increase production. Hence, any attempt by governments to boost labor supply, GDP or employment, by increasing money circulation cannot succeed and will merely cause, directly and proportionally, inflation.

Third, if it seems to you that all is very much on the back of workers, you are right. The logical structure of neoclassical economics put on laborers all the economy's motion. According to the theory, the will of workers is even responsible for long-lasting unemployment. There are two types of unemployment, voluntary and frictional. The latter happens because of market maladjustments, such as geographical mismatches between labor supply and demand, temporary dealignment of skills, and bureaucratic obstacles. That said, frictional unemployment is only temporary and lasts as long as it takes to solve the frictions hindering the working of the labor market.

On the other hand, voluntary unemployment is not temporary. Neoclassical economics considers it the most common type of unemployment. Workers are fully responsible for it, because of their slothful behavior, which hampers real wage diminishments. If workers were prepared to have their work disutility bought by lower real wages, this would ensure greater entrepreneurial demand for them. But workers are not so easy-breezy, neoclassical believed. To make matters worse, workers join themselves in powerful unions, resulting in wages that became tougher to reduce.

Why do businesspeople not accept workers' demand for higher real wages and satisfy themselves with lower profits? Because lesser profits would not pay what they consider to be a fair remuneration for their capital. But observe that this entrepreneurial behavior is nothing but a response to the state of things prevailing in the labor market, where workers have already defined the conditions of the game for the whole supply-led economy. There was no involuntary unemployment in neoclassical economics. Apart from the temporary frictional unemployment, all idleness in the workforce existed because of laborers' reluctance to admit a wage reduction that would stimulate businesspeople's demand for more employees.

To sum up, from postulate (2) various theoretical outcomes emerge within neoclassical economics. They are (1) equilibrium in all markets, (2) Say's law, (3) the supply-side economics, (4) the interest rate as a reward for waiting that balances the loanable funds market, (5) savings preceding investment, (6) money neutrality, (7) money supply causing inflation (neoclassical money quantity theory), and (8) voluntary employment as the permanent unemployment type. It may seem as though Keynes has made all this up, but he did not. He had been taught this theory and for years he taught it. He knew neoclassical economics extremely well. But as time went on and he encountered the Great War, Central European hyperinflation, 1929's Great Depression, and approached the edge of a second global war from the mid-1930s, Keynes first realized and then showed that neoclassical economics was deeply wrong.

Keynes' Checkmate

Keynes decided not merely to counter the neoclassical perspective with his own theory but also to demonstrate fundamental flaws in neoclassical's theory underpinnings. Therefore, he began his movements with an exposition and explanation of neoclassical economics, allowing him to criticize the theory and expose its fragilities. As you have just seen, postulate (2) backs many theoretical elements in neoclassical economics; thus, Keynes targeted it in his checkmate strategy. He launched three criticisms of the second postulate (using induction as his method for uncovering the flaws).

His first objection to the neoclassical theory attacked its claims that workers do not accept reduced nominal wages because this, given the price level, will lower real wages and instantaneously shift labor utility. In view of that, Keynes inducted his criticism through an analogy and showed an inconsistency in the neoclassical viewpoint. He created an analogy, which he considered a submethod of induction, and assumed the same changing real wages as neoclassical economics but through different means.

Keynes' analogy was the following. He assumed constant nominal salaries but moved prices up; real wages then decrease, like they do as nominal salaries move down, but prices remain constant. But in fact, given nominal salaries, inflation decreasing real wages happens all the time. Yet do people quit jobs in response to these changes in their real wages? Does unemployment grow just because from one month to another consumer prices increased but salaries did not? The answer to these questions is no. Keynes therefore concluded that real wages do not explain labor supply.

The second objection: based on a big amount of evidence delivered by the facts of experience, Keynes induced that workers, unionized or not, do not contract real wages. Nor do they contract nominal wages subject to change in short time periods, as neoclassical economists theorized. Employees and employers agree on nominal wages in work contracts, which are, in fact, rigid for some time. Sticky wage contracts are the rule in the job market – thus they are the sort of salary contract that Keynes adopted in *The General Theory*. He also added that workers have a range of real wages they want, perhaps set relatively to both other workers and a certain desired lifestyle. But laborers do not agree to supply their workforce with a unique real wage; they do not behave in such a take-it-or-leave-it manner. They are unlikely to know the prevalent real wage in the market and, to get a job or continue employed, they accept various real wages. Once again, real wages do not determine labor supply.

The third objection: in neoclassical economics, workers not only set their real wages but also set the volume of employment. Workers, unionized or not, have such power that they can define price (wage) and quantity (employment level) in the labor market. It is as if their individual behavior were so well coordinated that could make workers a kind of monopoly that has full market control. Keynes, again inducing by the facts of experience, argued that workers were not so powerful.

By the 1930s, when Keynes questioned neoclassical economics, simply looking out the window would show lines of people seeking jobs. But they were not queuing to refuse some real wage that did not compensate them for their utility. Workers were neither as futile nor as powerful as neoclassical economics assumed them to be. Keynes strongly objected to this neoclassical view. He stated that workers were not price and quantity makers, but price and quantity *takers*. Yet again, the neoclassical theory did not match the economic facts, let alone explain them.

The only situation in which workers could, perhaps, have the power that neoclassical economics ascribed to them is full employment. This is the very particular case in which neoclassical economics would work. But it is only a particular case; its absence is the general case in the economy, and in this general case, real wages do not drive the supply of the workforce. Moreover, working contracts are penned in nominal terms and the contracted monetary salaries are sticky; they do not change as quickly as inflation reduces real wages. Finally, workers are not the strongest, but the *weakest* side of the labor market.

The neoclassical theoretical building fell apart when Keynes checkmated postulate (2). Real wages do not explain labor supply. And if they do not, the neoclassical theory is insufficient to explain the labor market. Therefore, neoclassical economics is unable to explain the general case of the economy, unemployment. Thus another theory is needed. With his *The General Theory*, Keynes addressed the lack of a theory that could explain the economic system in its most general circumstance.

Before we finish this chapter, let us briefly explore three further points. First, if not by real wages, how did Keynes explain labor supply? He advanced a number of elements to justify labor supply, which can be split into two categories. First are characteristics of the country's population, like its size, age, working habits, labor capacity (in today's jargon, human capital), and even its degree of labor disutility. The second are economic conditions of the country, such as the technical state of its productive structure, how rich the country is, and how its wealth is distributed.

Second, we have not said much about the first postulate so far; what about it? Keynes accepted it as undeniably true. Real wages are part of the product that belongs to workers. If the country's GDP is $10, and $5 is the sum of wages, then $5 is the wage share of the GDP and the other $5 is profits. A country's income necessarily goes to the pockets of those who produced it. This is the logic of the first postulate. However, even having judged its logic to be true, Keynes did not transform the first postulate on entrepreneurs' demand for workers as neoclassical economics did. Keynes explained that entrepreneurial demand for employees depends on other reasons (which we will explore in the next chapters).

Finally, if neoclassical economics cannot explain the economy, the unemployment types it describes (frictional and voluntary) are no longer the only ones possible. Keynes accepted the existence of both cases, but they were not the most common unemployment type. The most general sort of unemployment is involuntary unemployment, a concept that Keynes created. He said that

> men are involuntarily unemployed if, in the event of a small rise in the price of wage-goods relatively to the money-wage, both the aggregate supply of labour willing to work for the current money-wage and the aggregate demand for it at that wage would be greater than the existing volume of employment.
>
> *(Keynes, 2013d, p. 14)*

In the quote, Keynes made an analogy to the neoclassical view on unemployment in order to define involuntary unemployment. It is the case that, independent of reductions in real wages, people still look for jobs and accept the current pay the labor market offers, yet no demand for their workforce exists. They *want* to work, but businesspeople are not interested in hiring them. Involuntary unemployment is the most general and common economic problem, and Keynes explained it in his *The General Theory of Employment, Interest and Money*. What explains employment? We account for that in our next chapter.

References

Keynes, J. M. (2013d). *The General Theory of Employment, Interest and Money: The Collected Writings of John Maynard Keynes*, vol. VII. London: Royal Economic Society and Cambridge University Press.

Pigou, A. C. (1933). *The Theory of Employment*. London: Macmillan.

6

IF NOT NEOCLASSICAL SUPPLY-SIDE ECONOMICS, THEN WHAT? KEYNES' DEMAND-SIDE ECONOMICS

The last chapter showed that Keynes choose to attack the second postulate of neoclassical economics because it structured much of its theoretical edifice. His strategy to challenge neoclassical economics focused on meticulously explaining it in order to develop an internal criticism of the theory, demonstrating its logical and factual problems. Keynes struck the second postulate so hard that neoclassical partisans could not fix it afterward. Together with the second postulate, the entire neoclassical building collapsed: Say's law and its full employment supply-side economics became senseless.

With neoclassical economics struck down, Keynes offered his demand-side economics to make up for the lack of a theory that could explain the economic system. *The General Theory*'s Chapter 3 unpacks the principle of effective demand and Keynes' demand-side economics. This effective demand principle disentangles the unanswered question with which the last chapter finished: what explains employment?

Keynes started *The General Theory*'s Chapter 3 by explaining aggregate supply. This is the whole production of the economy or, in the well-known acronym, its GDP. It starts with businesspeople resolving to establish a productive process that must employ workers to bring about goods and services. Thus, the physical extent of aggregate supply depends on the workers producing it. In mathematical parlance, Keynes penned the aggregate supply as follows:

$$\text{Aggregate supply} = f(N).$$

This means that aggregate supply functions because of employment, N, much as cars function because of fuel. In simpler words, employment N explains the physical extent of aggregate supply. If it is employment that produces the aggregate supply, the existence of the latter always owns to the former. Even if we think of

DOI: 10.4324/9781003287094-10

a machine or a device functioning through artificial intelligence, before it could work autonomously, there was a person manufacturing it. This is what the afore-mentioned function signifies, workers produce everything.

Do you remember that Keynes conceived capitalism as the monetary economy of production? Thus, money matters and Keynes also advanced a transformed ver-sion of the aforementioned function, displaying it in monetary terms. He called it the price of aggregate supply, which is the GDP expressed in terms of money. A simple example helps. Our chapter's one Brazilian ice-creamer produces 20 cans of ice-cream; this is her physical production. If she sells each can for $1, the price of her individual supply is $20. If all entrepreneurs in the country produce 1,000 physical units of goods and services and sell them for $1 each, the price of aggregate supply is $1,000.

By the way, let us deviate a bit from our route to give a hint that can make your reading of *The General Theory* easy. When reading this book, you will notice Keynes saying *unit of wages* to specify monetary terms; as wages are paid in money, a unit of wage logically translates itself into some amount of money. Moreover, as a worker is employed to produce a quantity of something, another unit of meas-urement that Keynes used in the book was the *unit of labor*; it measures physical quantities. Therefore, a unit of labor is employed and receives a unit of wage, so a unit of quantity and its monetary correspondence are specified. The third unit that Keynes adopted was the *unit of time*. It makes references to some point in time, such as the past, present, and future. Keep in mind that time in *The General Theory* is historical, it runs through calendars. As discussed earlier, it is not the logical type of time assumed by neoclassical economics. Therefore, when you read *The General Theory*, bear in mind these three units that Keynes used, namely, units of wage, labor, and time.

Let us resume the explanation of the determinants of employment. Business-people initiate productive processes because they wish to receive their supply price (i.e., the proceeds of their sales). When our ice-cream producer displays 20 ice-cream cans, vending each for $1, her intention is to earn these $20. These earnings will both pay for the employment she added and compensate her with some profit. The same reasoning holds for the *aggregate* supply price. It is the proceeds all busi-nesspeople in the economy desire when they employ workers, produce goods and services, and offer them to the economy. Producers are not searching for physical units; what they want are the monetary gains coming from the physical product. The latter is just a means for entrepreneurs to make more money than they invested to start production. Only because of this desire, the fulfillment of which requires production, do they agree to employ workers.

Whereas the neoclassical story is initiated by workers' willingness to voluntarily supply their labor (or not), Keynes' view is quite different. We have been talking about aggregate supply, but it does not result from workers offering their labor. Aggregate supply is the outcome of entrepreneurs kicking off productive processes. However, before any supply of goods and services begins, there must be demand in the form of investment. Investment is a component of demand. Demand creates supply and not the other way round, as neoclassical economists believed.

Therefore, the economic system is demand-led. Keynes delivered the script of this economic plot twist. He showed logical and factual problems within supply-side neoclassical economics that nullified its explicative power. He then explained that, in fact, supply was a creation of demand since production only exists because investments were made to create it. In addition, investment generates employment of workers. But why do entrepreneurs invest, employ, and produce?

As our ice-creamer exemplifies, entrepreneurs produce because they want to profit; vending goods and services they spawn is the means of reaching that goal. Demand plays a key role here too. If entrepreneurs only invest, employ, and produce because they want to sell their output, what obviously drives investment is the demand they expect for their production. A businessperson only employs workers in response to some expected demand. Accordingly, entrepreneurs engage in the level of employment that corresponds with the demand they expect for their production.

Hence, Keynes developed an aggregate demand function to set the relationship between demand and employment. This function states that the employment level created by entrepreneurs is an expression of the aggregate demand they expect for their production. The aggregate demand function shows, in Keynes' words, "the proceeds entrepreneurs expect to receive from the employment of N" (2013d, p. 25). Remember that N stands for employment, such as in the aggregate supply function; thereby,

$$\text{Aggregate demand} = f(N).$$

Our ice-creamer production also helps here. If she employed, say, two workers to produce 20 ice-creams, it was because she anticipated selling these 20 units. With each can sold for $1, she expected a monetary price of demand equal to $20. Hence, the monetary price of demand is the prospective monetary value entrepreneurs hope to gain. Our producer would have added two more workers if she had expected a 40-unit demand, rendering her a monetary demand price of $40. However, no people employed would mean no expectations of demand.

The same reasoning holds for *aggregate* demand. The employment of N workers explains an expected aggregate demand and produces an aggregate supply. Both aggregate supply and aggregate (that is, expected) demand have the same total monetary aggregate price. However, does the expected aggregate demand always equal a true, effective demand that precisely matches the aggregate supply? The answer to this question is no.

The effective demand is the demand that really happens, the actual, true demand that businesspeople face. It can be smaller, bigger, or equal to the expected aggregate demand they anticipated when they hired employees to produce the aggregate supply. The case in which effective demand is smaller than expected aggregate demand is the normal economic situation; it is the general case of monetary economies of production. The case where effective demand is larger than expected aggregate demand sometimes happens – for example, during economic booms – but it is uncommon. The last case, in which effective and aggregate demand precisely meet, is very rare. It occurs by "accident or design" (Keynes, 2013d, p. 28).

Let us summarize the reasoning advanced so far. Entrepreneurs invest and create a level of employment due to an aggregate demand that they expect and on account of which they produce an aggregate supply. However, what really matters after these N employees produce an output is effective demand. This will determine if the economy confirms the level of hiring by entrepreneurs. An effective demand that is insufficient to secure the aggregate supply means that the economy did not validate the employment level that businesspeople hired previously. The very rare balance between the effective demand and aggregate supply is an employment equilibrium point in which entrepreneurs are indifferent in maintaining their current position or adding workers to expand their production (if they believe in better future demand). Excessive effective demand in relation to aggregate supply (which happens during an economic boom boosted by credit boom, for instance) not only confirms businesspeople's employment level N but also encourages them to keep hiring. Hence, when effective demand intersects aggregate supply, the former indicates the level of employment (and production) that the economy really wants.

Think of it dynamically. First, entrepreneurs employ N workers because they await a certain aggregate demand, whereupon they engage these N workers to produce the aggregate supply. Employment has been created in this process, but so far it is only a gamble by entrepreneurs. Then, production is delivered in markets and effective demand sets the point at which entrepreneurs' bids were correct. This is the principle of effective demand. It explains the level of employment in Keynes' demand-led economics. Consequently, to fully understand employment, we must go deeper into the components of demand.

Keynes set a simple framework in *The General Theory*, with only two agents: families and firms (in this book, we have also been calling families *individuals* or *agents*, and firms *companies*, which are led by *entrepreneurs* or *businesspeople* and we will continue doing so in the next chapters). Thus, demand has two components, consumption and investment. He chose this simple scheme because he was especially eyeing private investment and its fluctuations over time. Governments and the external sector are surely important parts of demand. But in free-initiative capitalism, Keynes saw private investment as the most important economic act; it is society's wealth constructor. Consumption has the essential role of securing part of the product that investment created. But even when people consume, they can do so because some investment happened beforehand such that the entrepreneurs' invested wealth became income to those they employed.

Let us have a look at these two components of demand, consumption and investment. Our foray into the determinants of investment and consumption here is more general and intended to provide an overview. In the next chapters, we delve deeper into both and fully explain their determinants.

Consumption, the Fundamental Psychological Law, and Investment

Economic dynamics starts with demand in the form of investment. In monetary economies of production, investment means money expenditure to employ workers and to buy capital assets to build productive processes. The wealth businesspeople invest becomes income to those who receive it, that is, to workers and other businesspeople who supply inputs to the production initiated by the entrepreneur. Income, in turn, explains consumption; in simpler words, consumption only functions because of income:

Aggregate consumption $= f(\text{Income})$.

The chain is: investment creates production and income and all that entrepreneurs expect is that those who receive the latter demand the former. They hope that income return to their pockets through people consuming their supply. Keynes named *propensity to consume* that part of income that becomes consumption. This chain can also be seen dynamically. New investments create new income that, consequently, generates more consumption. Keynes called this dynamic change of consumption arising from new income the *marginal propensity to consume*. It dictates the part of the new income that is converted into new consumption. The higher the marginal propensity to consume, the larger the consumed part of new income and vice versa. Let the reader bear in mind that, in economic jargon, *marginal* means movement from one point to another, like from one quarter to another, a month to another, or a year to another. The marginal propensity to consume is thus the change in consumption from the previous moment to the new one, following a variation in the level of income.

However, based on the facts of experience, Keynes induced a fundamental psychological law about the marginal propensity to consume. Although consumers always increase consumption following a rise in income, on average, aggregate income increases more than aggregate consumption. Therefore, consumption grows as income increases, but the latter expands more than the former. Hence, along with higher income, greater savings emerge. But bigger savings imply smaller effective demand, threatening businesspeople's expectations.

Effective demand must validate the employment and production that entrepreneurs decided to create. The new production necessarily has the same value as the new income. However, this new income is larger than its resulting new consumption; accordingly, the new consumption is necessarily smaller than the new production. The fundamental psychological law implies that consumption is incapable of effectively demanding the whole production. On its own, consumption would not sustain the level of employment selected by entrepreneurs; thereby, unemployment equivalent to the size of society's savings would occur, pushing employment persistently downward.

What could make effective demand equal to aggregate supply? Investment is responsible for this. In addition to consumption, investment is the component of demand that can effectively secure the non-consumed part of production. More than simply igniting economic dynamics, investment is also ultimately responsible for keeping effective demand and aggregate supply in equilibrium. Accordingly, it accounts for the stability and growth of employment.

Investment has two determinants. The first is the marginal efficiency of capital, which is the rate of return over the costs, or capital assets' internal rate of return. The second determinant is the interest rate, which is the alternative return that entrepreneurs can obtain if they invest in financial assets. However, as repeatedly said, financial assets do not directly create employment; some of them never create a job.

Investment needs to occupy the demand gap that savings create, but investment and savings have different determinants. Aggregate income defines savings. Investment, in turn, is determined by two return rates, the marginal efficiency of capital and the interest rate. This explains Keynes' saying that investment equals savings only by accident or design. It is rare for investment to make effective demand precisely equal to the aggregate supply. Consequently, economies frequently suffer from insufficient effective demand. This causes involuntary unemployment and, sometimes, crises, recessions, and depressions. Different from neoclassical economics, interest rates for Keynes do not balance investment and savings, nor do savings precede investments. Quite the opposite, in Keynes' demand-led economics, investment creates savings as it forges income and production.

To conclude, a recap. Entrepreneurs employ when they invest based on some expected aggregate demand in response to which they produce an aggregate supply. Entrepreneurs wish to profit through selling their supply; for that, they need effective demand for their production. This is Keynes' demand-led economics. Whereas entrepreneurs' initial employment is a gamble, a conjecture on how much society would demand, the effective demand is concrete and defines the employment that society actually supports. Effective demand can be smaller, bigger, or balanced with the employment level that entrepreneurs previously created. This is the effective demand principle, and employment varies according to it.

Consumption and investment form effective demand. Aggregate income determines the former. The consumed amount of income depends on society's propensity to consume, which grows when income increases but at a decreasing rate. Thus, consumption rises along with the expansion of investments, production, and income, but so do savings. This is the fundamental psychological law that Keynes inferred from the facts of experience. It means that a gap in effective demand in relation to aggregate supply occurs whenever production increases. But this gap, caused by savings, frustrates entrepreneurs' expectations and is likely to make them fire workers, increasing unemployment. In the end, investment becomes responsible for filling the gap between effective demand and aggregate supply; employment follows the lead. This is Keynes' general theory of employment. The next chapters separate out the determinants of effective demand, dealing first with consumption and then with investment.

Reference

Keynes, J. M. (2013d). *The General Theory of Employment, Interest and Money: The Collected Writings of John Maynard Keynes*, vol. VII. London: Royal Economic Society and Cambridge University Press.

7
DEMAND EXPLAINED

Consumption

As we spoke of in the last chapter, income explains consumption. The logic is straightforward: people can consume only if they have income. People can save money out of their income and dissave it later to consume if, for example, they lose their jobs. Although dissaving can fund consumption, the former, inescapably, only exists after previous income provided people with the power of saving. Income, in turn, is generated as entrepreneurs invested their wealth and made money circulate throughout the economy, igniting the economic dynamics.

Most businesspeople engage in investments that produce goods for consumption as consumption usually is the main component of demand. In the United States, for instance, private expenditures of households in consumption accounted for 68% of the US GDP in December 2021, whereas in the United Kingdom, consumption was 63.8% of the GDP, 64.3% in Brazil, 63.6% in South Africa, 50.7% in Australia, 49.7% in Germany, 46.2% in South Korea, and 37.8% in China. Export-leading countries, like Germany, South Korea, Australia, and China, have smaller shares of their GDP as private consumption and greater shares of exports. Nevertheless, consumption is still a major component of demand.

As the last chapter advanced, Keynes called propensity to consume the share of income which becomes consumption. It is the average level of consumption made from the whole income received by all social classes in the country. Wealthier classes have lower propensity to consume because richer individuals have their material needs satisfied already. Accordingly, the wealthier the country, the smaller its propensity to consume.

Another important concept that Keynes pointed out, and the last chapter also brought it about, is the marginal propensity to consume. It gives the dynamics of the propensity to consume (it is never too much to repeat that when economists say *margin* they refer to some movement from one point to another, like from last year to today or from September to October). Investments always create new income,

DOI: 10.4324/9781003287094-11

and the marginal propensity to consume explains the share of the new rent that is converted into new consumption. While the propensity to consume sets the aggregate consumption level, the marginal propensity to consume states how much consumption varies around this level.

For instance, it is like velocity and acceleration. Velocity is the propensity to consume, and acceleration is the marginal propensity to consume. Acceleration is the flow that changes the stock of velocity. A car is faster as its acceleration rapidly pushes up its velocity. However, as speed grows due to a fast flow of acceleration, the engine of the car gets close to its full capacity. This means that acceleration is still positive, but it now has a decreasing rate that sustains, but without increasing, velocity. In analogy, this is the relation between the propensity to consume (the consumed share of income) and the marginal propensity to consume (the dynamic flow (rate) at which income variations cause shifts in consumption).

Thus, the marginal propensity to consume pushes the propensity to consume over time. This movement is faster the bigger it is the marginal propensity to consume. A lower marginal propensity to consume underlies an already high aggregate propensity to consume, which is typical of rich countries. In this case, aggregate consumption would not change much over time. The opposite holds for poor- and medium-income countries. It is worth mentioning that the inverse of the marginal propensity to consume is the marginal propensity to save. When individuals, firms, and governments define their consumption, they residually decide their savings.

In Chapters 8 and 9 of *The General Theory*, Keynes explained the factors conditioning the propensity to consume. He separated them into objective and subjective factors. The first are those related to variations in income, and the latter consists of the elements that constitute the number assumed by the marginal propensity to consume. A simple mathematical parlance helps report the meaning of the objective and subjective factors defining the propensity to consume. Let us recall the consumption function:

Aggregate consumption $= f(\text{Income})$.

Following Keynes' theory of consumption, we restate this function into its complete form:

Aggregate consumption $= c_0 + c_1(\text{Income})$.

This equation means that aggregate income explains aggregate consumption and bears a positive relationship with it; hence, when income increases, consumption also does so. Variable c_0 is the autonomous consumption, which is the consumption made when the consumer has no income. This demand can be financed by dissaving, borrowing from banks, family, or friends, or vending patrimony priorly accumulated. In turn, c_1 is the marginal propensity to consume. It shows how consumption shifts following a change in income.

For instance, Toneto, Ribas, and Carvalho (2021) calculated the 2017–2018 value of c_1, the marginal propensity to consume, for different classes of wealth in Brazil. For the poorest 10% of Brazilians, the marginal propensity to consume was 0.869, out of each new R\$1 of income, R\$0.869 was consumed. The richest 50–60% of the population consumed R\$0.679 out of each R\$1 new income. The marginal propensity to consume of the wealthiest 1% equaled 0.237: they only spent R\$0.23 cents from each new R\$1 they gained. On average, the 2017–2018 Brazilian marginal propensity to consume was 0.657.

The objective factors defining the propensity to consume are the elements that change income. The subjective factors form the coefficient c_1; in simpler words, they set the number called marginal propensity to consume. Keynes listed, in Chapter 8 of *The General Theory*, six objective factors conditioning the propensity to consume. In Chapter 9, he enrolled other 12 subjective factors that define the marginal propensity to consume.

The objective factors that cause income to vary are as follows:

(1) Changes in income
(2) Changes in the difference between gross and net income
(3) Windfall capital gains – like those coming from increasing market prices of securities, bonds, and equities
(4) Changes in the intertemporal rate of discount; this is the difference of consumption today in relation to future consumption (in economic jargon, money opportunity cost over time). This cost is measured by gains you can have by investing your money in financial assets rather than using it to consume. If interest rates are high, current consumption becomes more expensive because of the opportunity of yielding interest by quitting consumption, saving, and buying financial assets. Keynes also warned that the opportunity cost of allocating consumption over time must not only account for the foreseen gains, but they should also include all risks involving the passage of time, including the chance of not being alive in the future and thus not enjoying future earnings.
(5) Changes in fiscal policy – which come from different taxation and/or shifts in public expenditures.
(6) Changes in the expected relation between current and future income – Keynes explained that uncertainty would make this factor inexpressive for aggregate consumption, but he recognized that for some individuals, especially those employed in steady jobs, it could be important.

The 12 factors molding the marginal propensity to consume, and so defining the flow of novel income which becomes new consumption, are divided into reasons of individuals, firms, and governments. For individuals, these factors are as follows:

(1) Precaution – individuals hold a reserve for unforeseen events.
(2) Foresight – individuals abstain from consuming and save to build a reserve for the future.

(3) Calculation – individuals might consume less today as they want to take advantage of interest and capital gains to accumulate wealth and consume more in the future.
(4) Improvement – even at the cost of a smaller present joy, individuals might prefer to slowly increase their consumption over time, since this may satisfy those who search for a gradual improvement in their standard of living.
(5) Independence – individuals can save money to be free to do whatever they want, even if they do not know what this want would be.
(6) Enterprise – if individuals want to take advantage of profitable opportunities, they must have resources. Savings provide them with these.
(7) Pride – individuals might want to bequeath a fortune. Less consumption throughout their lives can make this fortune, to be forsaken to their heirs.
(8) Avarice – as Keynes explained "to satisfy pure miserliness, i.e., unreasonable but insistent inhibitions against acts of expenditure as such" (2013d, p. 108).

To these eight subjective factors, Keynes added another four that drive firms' and governments' marginal propensity to consume. These other factors are as follows:

(1) Enterprise – firms and governments might save resources to self-finance further investments they plan to realize.
(2) Liquidity – liquidity is firms and governments securing resources to confront contingencies, such as the aforementioned precaution that individuals do.
(3) Improvement – such as for individuals, this factor implies saving now in exchange for better future conditions. However, firms and governments that make big current savings might be seen, Keynes alerted, as having good management, even if the accumulated resources result from savings and not from more efficiency. Thus, the improvement factor can sometimes be exercised to protect public and private managers from criticisms.
(4) Financial prudence – it is the anticipated provision of resources to discharge debt and write off capital goods' costs of wastage and obsolescence.

Keynes figured out these motives knowing that they were not exhaustive, but indicative. More factors can be added to the list, which will always be changing over time. Moreover, Keynes argued that objective factors are liable to short-term variations. However, the subjective ones are stabler as they depend on society's economic institutions and organizations which, in turn, relies on habits formed from religion, education, moral, history, wealth distribution, technology, and so on. In normal conditions, the underlying elements of the subjective factors change secularly, and thus the propensity to consume switches slowly.

Nevertheless, there is another essential element related to the marginal propensity to consume, which associates consumption with investment: the investment multiplier. Keynes borrowed it from Richard Khan, his pupil at Cambridge, and inserted it in *The General Theory*. Keynes gave it such a highlight that the multiplier got a chapter of its own. Let us have a look at it.

The Multiplier of Investments

The multiplier measures the flow of money circulating in the economy after an investment is made. Although Keynes adopted it emphasizing how an investment would multiplicate income, the multiplier is commonly seen in terms of employment. Whenever a big investment is made, news noticing it reports how many direct, or primary jobs, and secondary, indirect jobs the venture will generate. These two rounds of job creation come from one single investment. Therefore, investment multiplies employment. It also does so with income. Each $1 invested multiplies income to more than $1. Why is that? Because of the marginal propensity to consume and the circuit of money expenditure that it propels in the economy.

For instance, an investment hires worker A for, say, $1 and this $1 investment spending is worker A's income. Let us assume that this society has a marginal propensity to consume of 0.90, on average. So, worker A receives $1 and consumes $0.90 from entrepreneur B, whose proceeds of $0.90 promptly turn into a $0.81 consumption from supplier C, who earns this $0.81 and consumes $0.73 from producer D. An investment of $1 became an income of $1 for worker A, proceeds of $0.90 to entrepreneur B, and a rent of $0.81 to supplier C and D's $0.73 rent. In the end, an investment of $1 generated an income of $3.44. This is the multiplier effect. The bigger it is the marginal propensity to consume, the larger the multiplier will be. The underlying logic of the multiplier is that a large marginal propensity to consume makes a major part of an income generated by an investment turn back to the economy as consumption.

Nevertheless, a big marginal propensity to consume might not be enough to activate a great multiplier. Keynes listed factors that limit its working, such as the capacity of industries that produce capital goods to foresee an investment boom (the faster the boom is outlooked, the better); the employment level (a lower unemployment makes the multiplier greater but it also limits the possible expansion of supply); the share of imports complementing the country's aggregate supply (the bigger imports, the smaller the multiplier); the share of investments in effective demand (the larger this share, the greater the multiplier); and the response of prices to the decrease in unemployment (if prices increase faster than wages, businesspeople gain more, but their smaller marginal propensity to consume reduces the multiplier).

Keynes also debated how government spending and the multiplier are associated. If the public is unconfident about the government, even in a society bearing a big marginal propensity to consume, the multiplier might be limited and not work as actively as it would if people trusted the government. Therefore, if people doubt the government, they increase their precautions, save money, and, consequently, the multiplier gets lower. But a government that inspires public trust can be helpful in stabilizing the economy in crisis or stagnation. In this case, public spending would make money circulate in the economy; thus, it would activate the multiplier and foster a better economic dynamic.

To conclude, consumption is a major component of effective demand, and so most businesspeople invest to produce consumption goods. Investment generates income, and the latter explains consumption. The portion of income that turns back to the economy as consumption relies on the propensity to consume. The marginal propensity to consume, in turn, explains the movement of the propensity to consume over time because it determines how much of new income becomes new consumption – whereby it also defines the investment multiplier.

However, we learned the fundamental psychological law in the last chapter, which Keynes induced from the facts of experience. The law asserts that variations in income are always greater than variations in consumption. Thus, whenever investment, production, and income increase, consumption goes up too, but to a smaller degree. The gap between production and effective demand must be filled by the other component of demand, namely, investment. Thereupon, investment is explained in the next chapter.

References

Keynes, J. M. (2013d). *The General Theory of Employment, Interest and Money: The Collected Writings of John Maynard Keynes*, vol. VII. London: Royal Economic Society and Cambridge University Press.

Toneto, R., Ribas, T. and Carvalho, L. (2021). *Nota de Economia Política do MADE*. Centro de Pesquisa em Macroeconomia das Desigualdades 008. São Paulo: MADE-Universidade de São Paulo.

8

DEMAND EXPLAINED

Investment

The importance of investment in Keynes' monetary economy of production is twofold. First, investment stimulates economic activity, generating employment, income, and production. However, increases in income are not followed by equivalent elevations in consumption; the latter grows on a smaller scale than the former, so when income swells, bigger savings emerge. The second importance of investment is that it demands that part of the aggregate supply that was not initially consumed. Long story short: investment is responsible for both pushing the economy and keeping it stable over time. Economic stability means an effective demand that is sufficient to match the aggregate supply, resulting in entrepreneurs at least carrying on at the employment level they previously created.

We have been talking about investment since the beginning of the book, first in the investment decision-making model outlined in Chapter 1 and, further, in Chapter 4 discussion of *A Treatise on Money*. Moreover, Keynes' investment theory was an important element in the effective demand principle, presented in Chapter 6. Chapter 6 also pointed out the two variables that determine investment, namely, the marginal efficiency of capital and the interest rate. Here, we go through the first of these determinants and, in the next chapter, address the interest rate.

As a reminder, by investment, we mean productive investment. As Chapter 4 explained, investment is the purchase of capital assets, also called capital goods or capital equipment, that produce other goods and services during their lifespan. Businesspeople only buy capital goods because they believe that selling their production will furnish them with prospective yields throughout the life cycle of the equipment they acquired. Put simply, entrepreneurs buy capital goods and employ workers to operate them, pursuing the prospective yields, net of operational costs, that they expect to gain vending their production.

We should be insistent on one point. Lest the readers understand prospective yields as current proceeds, they are not. These gains are expected in the future,

DOI: 10.4324/9781003287094-12

and they are not an expectation of rent gained once and for all. The expectation is that the yields will last however long the capital asset endures. They are prospective because they are taken with a view to the future.

The feasibility of an investment depends on a comparison between the net prospective yields of the capital asset and the cost of purchasing that asset. This cost can be seen as the supply price of the capital asset. This is the price at which its manufacturer agrees to produce a new unit of capital equipment and sell it to an entrepreneur willing to start or expand a productive process. As always in economics, the price at which the seller supplies something is the cost to the buyer. In this case, the cost of acquiring capital goods is the investment cost.

How is the comparison between net prospective yields and investment cost carried out? The answer to this is given by the marginal efficiency of capital, a mathematical ratio that is a determinant of investment. Its numerator is the sum of all prospective net yields expected by entrepreneurs as proceeds from the capital goods they acquired. The supply price of the capital asset, which is the entrepreneur's investment cost, is the ratio's denominator. In more approachable mathematical language, assuming time as a specific period such as a month, quarter, semester, or year, the marginal efficiency of capital is:

$$= \frac{expected\ prospective\ yield_{time\,1} + expected\ prospective\ yield_{time\,2} + \cdots + expected\ prospective\ yield_{time\,n}}{Investment\ cost\left(or\ the\ supply\ price\ of\ the\ capital\ asset\right)}.$$

In current terminology, the marginal efficiency of capital is better known as the internal rate of return. Technically, this is the rate that brings the expected future yields to their present value and makes it possible the comparison between the present value of the prospective yields and the current supply price of the capital asset. The marginal efficiency of capital is thus a discount rate that links future values to their present amount. If the rate fetches a present value of future yields that at least equals the cost of the capital asset, the investment is worthwhile (assuming, for the sake of simplicity, that all other relevant variables remain constant).

We can explain the logic of the marginal efficiency of capital by analogy with the interest rate, which is the other determinant of investment. Instead of discounting future values into a present value, as the marginal efficiency of capital does, think in the opposite direction: the capitalization of a present value into a greater future amount. This is the case when an interest rate is paid on a set amount of money over time. The motivation for buying a financial asset that is capitalized into a greater future value is the same as when entrepreneurs buy capital goods: they wish to make more money than that they had before. As such, both the marginal efficiency of capital and interest rate are rates of return on assets. Being comparable rates of return, these two variables determinate investment.

However, whereas a fixed-income financial asset allows investors to know the future value of their wealth, entrepreneurs cannot determine for sure the prospective yields compounding the marginal efficiency of their capital goods. A yet non-existent future cannot be a component of the set of direct knowledge, upon which entrepreneurs must make, in the present, their decision to invest. Therefore, prospective yields of capital goods cannot be known for certain; the future, the moment that reveals these proceeds, does not currently exist. If something cannot be learned, it is nothing but expectations.

As said when discussing *A Treatise on Probability*, Keynes sustained the argument that expectations are an unavoidable part of human reasoning. Therefore, expectations are an unavoidable factor in the calculus of the marginal efficiency of capital. Thus, entrepreneurs cannot help but use expectations to estimate prospective yields. Neither are expectations only related to the present time. Quite the opposite. They are a present imagining of the future, and they bridge these two moments that are economically never disconnected: the present and the future. The marginal efficiency of capital as a discount rate and the interest rate as a capitalization rate only provide yields over time. However, the decision to take a chance and invest in pursuit of one of these return rates is made in the present, based upon expectations of the future.

Keynes pointed out two types of expectations. Short-term expectations relate to decisions about existing capital goods. For instance, resolutions of price, production, employment of workers to operate an active equipment, and shifts to be worked are all decisions relying on short-term expectations. Long-term expectations are those taken into account in the marginal efficiency of capital. They ground decisions pertinent to acquiring a new capital asset. Hence, these expectations drive investment decisions.

Long-term expectations, Keynes explained, are partly formed by facts about which entrepreneurs are more or less certain and partly by expectations about the future, upon which entrepreneurs can only have more or less confidence but no certainty. Things known with relative certainty include, for instance, the average wage, GDP growth rate, unemployment level, demand for a specific product, and competition level. The suppositions about the future are the entrepreneurs' guesses, for instance, that they estimated the corrected level of demand for their products and that they hired the correct number of workers.

The short- and long-term expectations are surely intertwined. The short-term expectations involve facts entrepreneurs can fairly say they know and they can stimulate investment-relevant long-term expectations whenever businesspeople are met with an effective demand that satisfies their previous long-term expectations. Nevertheless, short- and long-term expectations are not the same thing. The first only applies to decisions about existing capital equipment because, at some point in the past, long-term expectations prompted businesspeople to purchase long-lasting capital goods.

Regarding the measurement of the marginal efficiency of capital, Keynes never rejected the idea that mathematical calculus could be used to improve the estimation of prospective yields. All tools available to collect information and furnish greater assistance to businesspeople are welcome – like consulting firms, broadcasts, and big data. However, as Keynes warned at length, a bigger informational set that establishes a robust mathematical estimation of the marginal efficiency of capital should not be taken by the decision-maker as affording absolute certainty. Such a thing does not exist.

In *The General Theory*, Keynes advanced the concept of the state of confidence, an updated name for the degree of rational belief from *A Treatise on Probability*. The state of confidence is businesspeople's subjective judgment about how much they believe in the correctness of their expectations. For example, assume that our ice-creamer of earlier examples is granted an extensive information set, based on well-developed mathematical and statistical data, about both the general economic situation of Brazil and the specifics of producing ice-cream in this country. Taking account of all these data, our ice-creamer calculates the marginal efficiency of her capital, which indicates that the expected prospective yields more than compensate for the present investment cost. Investing thus seems like a good idea. If her subjective and intuitive state of confident trusts in her expectations of selling the output of her production, she invests.

Nevertheless, in similar conditions, she may decide otherwise. Therefore, ice-cream will neither be made nor will laborers be hired. If there is a single factor of concern among the several that are favorable in the formation of her set of direct knowledge, and she overweighs that sole negative factor to mold her state of confidence, she refrains from investing. Hence, for investment decisions, it is not only expectations that matter but also the entrepreneurs' state of confidence in their expectations.

How much do entrepreneurs trust their expectations? How much do they regard them as either fragile or correct? Which factors weigh more or less than others in shaping their state of confidence? The answers to these questions can change depending on both the circumstances and how entrepreneurs consider these circumstances in their expectations. Accordingly, investment decisions are subject to volatility.

To support the formulation of expectations and strengthen the state of confidence, individuals create conventions. These are socially shared beliefs that become a component of the set of direct knowledge out of which expectations are formed. Although conventions can play this important role in the reasoning processes, they can, ironically, be based on beliefs rooted in other beliefs. Conventions need not be any actual or concrete evidence; sometimes, they may not be even tangible.

But if an idea emerges and social groups develop faith in that idea, making it last, it turns into a convention. Keynes mentioned a convention that usually prevails in economic decisions (and surely elsewhere) and nourishes people's state of confidence: the belief that the current situation will continue into the future (this convention can be undone if you contemplate how much things have changed during your own lifetime). Another example of convention is the well-known, mainly in analysis of the financial markets, bandwagon effect. It describes movements in which individuals intensely go in one direction because they share a common belief of either profiting or avoiding big losses if they follow the herd's lead. Keynes translated the idea surrounding the bandwagon effect into the maxim that people prefer to lose together to gain alone. As we shall soon see, some important economic aspects are conventions, like the interest rate and even money.

Based on elements like an individual's state of confidence and expectations, the decision to productively invest in a capital asset occurs, ultimately, owing to what Keynes named animal spirits, "a spontaneous urge to action rather than inaction, and not as the outcome of a weighted average of quantitative benefits multiplied by quantitative probabilities" (2013d, p. 161). Animal spirits explain why entrepreneurs confront the unknown and non-learnable time in pursuit of future prospective yields. In the end, the animal-spirits-based investment action is the driving force of economic dynamics. This entrepreneur's individual urge to action makes entrepreneurs invest, which generates the employment of workers as well as production, income, and social wealth. Therefore, an entrepreneur's individual animal spirits benefit the whole society.

The Challenges Confronting Investment (and, Consequently, Economic Activity)

Investment is volatile by nature as it is conditioned by elements too subjective and ethereal like expectations of prospective yields, state of confidence, and animal spirits. Nevertheless, Keynes also argued that two other factors could complicate a good investment trend. The first element is the fact that as aggregate investment increases over time, the marginal efficiency of capital in general decreases. Using the designation adopted by Keynes, the schedule of the marginal efficiency of capital, which is the aggregated marginal efficiency of capital of all individual investment plans, has an inverse relationship with the investment demand-schedule or, alternatively, aggregate investment. Whereas investment grows over time, its return falls. Two reasons explain this.

First, a boost in investment increases the supply price of capital goods. These are assets whose construction requires time for completion; they are not easy-to-replicate products like televisions, cars, or cookies. Moreover, they are specialized assets, constructed to serve the specific purposes of the entrepreneur by whom it was demanded. Hence, the capital goods industry, whenever confronted by higher investments, responds by raising prices. This, in turn, increases investment cost and lowers the marginal efficiency of capital. Keynes argued that this factor exerts its influence mostly in the short term.

The second reason for the inverse relationship described earlier concerns the scarcity of products in the long term. Products' exclusiveness, which is the market strategy to manage their availability, implies how high producers can set their price. Think of gold, for example. With its scant supply and an ongoing demand, gold's price continuously goes up in the long term, setting aside oscillations during crises. The same reasoning is true for several goods and services whose production is controlled by one or a few producers. When these producers create an atmosphere of exclusiveness in the access and use of their products, they are managing scarcity. Patents and the pursuit of innovations are attempts to build scarcity and exclusiveness, so that prices can be raised, leading to the greater marginal efficiency of capital. However, products with many producers face larger competition as they are easily substituted between brands; consequently, their prices and prospective yields go down.

But Keynes concluded that, in the long term, the scarcity of products would reduce as investment increased and raised the availability of goods and services, lowering producers' capacity to supply with exclusiveness. As a result, prices would decrease, reducing prospective yields and depressing the marginal efficiency of capital. For instance, observe how, over the years, the number of producers and our access to goods like mobile phones, televisions, smartwatches, and laptops have increased. The same holds for services. Notice how many suppliers of TV and music streaming, delivery apps, and social media now exist.

By the way, innovations are intended to surpass this decreasing scarcity over time. This is especially the case with radical innovations that produce a shift to a new a technological paradigm. Rather than refuting them, innovations confirm Keynes' views on the long-term downward tendency of prospective yields. Companies sprint for innovations in an attempt to increase their expected prospective yields from new products they create.

In sum, this first investment-disturbance factor can be understood by imagining an x and y graph on which the marginal efficiency of capital schedule is represented on the vertical y-axis, and the investment demand-schedule is plotted on the horizontal x-axis. The line connecting the dots between x and y has a downward slope, which means that the marginal efficiency of capital goes down as investment rises. First, in the short term, this is because increased investment elevates the price of capital goods. Second, in the long term, investment augments the aggregate supply of products, reducing their scarcity and prices, thereby depressing the marginal efficiency of capital.

The second investment-disrupting factor is the liquidity fetish. People are attracted by financial assets, like bonds, shares, and securities, because they are liquid, that is, they are more easily converted to money than capital goods. If these assets can expand personal wealth, why would entrepreneurs start a new business if they could buy an existing one through the stock market? Why would they confront the forces of uncertainty and time, immobilizing their wealth, if they could acquire equity in an already producing company and keep these liquid assets in their portfolio?

Financial markets developed with the intention of pooling resources from those who were not keen to manage a company but eager to fund it by making these resources available to those who wanted to establish a company but had no funds to do so. These were good intentions, Keynes argued. However, over time, the temptation to gain in the short term by gambling in liquid assets and without buying equipment and employing workers came to dominate. The liquidity fetish overruled and disturbed, if not subverted, the functioning of financial markets; it stimulated financialization, the era of wealth replication and accumulation through financial products. Several financial bubbles and crises better tell this history, including the Great Crash of 1929, which Keynes witnessed. The problem, however, is that financial crises are not watertight to financial markets. They depress expectations, credit, and businesses, leave workers unemployed, and destroy wealth; they thus strongly affect the real economy.

The logic behind financial dealings caught Keynes' attention. He criticized what is today known as day trading, that is, the purchase of a share in order to sell it hours later. He also illustrated a convention prevailing in financial markets using the metaphor of the beauty contest. Financial investors do not pay attention to the shares they assess as the best. They also disregard what they consider other investors will rate as the best shares. Rather, they go to a third level "where we devote our intelligence to anticipating what average opinion expects the average opinion to be" (2013d, p. 156). Let us remember that Keynes lived in a time much less interconnected than the present. Our online world magnifies the power of the liquidity fetish, which in turn promotes huge volatility in financial prices. Our current time then requires considerable animal spirits to encourage productive investments, but this is harder to find as financialization becomes increasingly widespread.

Nevertheless, financial markets, especially stock markets, became a sort of thermometer of economic activity. But the problem is that this thermometer oscillates in accordance with the convention described in the aforementioned paragraph, following the speculative behavior of market agents, whose expectations are aimed to bet on what the average expectation is ought to be and not to evaluate the true fundamentals of companies as well as of the economy. However, in order to build their expectations, entrepreneurs take into consideration how companies are assessed in stock markets, mainly those in the same business into which they are willing to invest. Consequently, stock markets driven by speculative purposes affect the measurement of the marginal efficiency of capital, having the power to encumber businesspeople's investment plans – and so cluttering the creation of more jobs and greater production.

Keynes explicitly differentiated speculative and enterprise activities. Speculation is typical of financial markets and refers to investors whose action seeks to only forecast what the average expectation of markets will be. They are only trying to anticipate the short-term psychology of the market in an attempt to move faster than the market, buying and selling shares before the other market agents. Enterprise, in turn, is the action of entrepreneurs. These businesspeople make productive investment, create jobs, and generate production and social wealth. Their challenge is to forecast prospective yields of capital goods throughout their lifespan and formulate the best possible measurement of the marginal efficiency of capital. These are the people imbued with animal spirits, upon which a good economic activity depends.

In addition to the marginal efficiency of capital, the interest rate also determines investment. Interest rates emerge from financial markets: thus, they are a monetary phenomenon. Their role as a determinant of investment makes it clear that the real and financial economic sectors are inseparable. To reveal the final elements of Keynes' *The General Theory of Employment, Interest and Money*, it is time to start exploring, in the next chapters, the two last nouns in the book's title, interest and money.

References

Keynes, J. M. (1921). *A Treatise on Probability*. London: Macmillan.

Keynes, J. M. (2013b). *A Treatise on Money I, the Pure Theory of Money: The Collected Writings of John Maynard Keynes*, vol. V. London: Cambridge University Press.

Keynes, J. M. (2013c). *A Treatise on Money II, the Applied Theory of Money: The Collected Writings of John Maynard Keynes*, vol. VI. London: Cambridge University Press.

Keynes, J. M. (2013d). *The General Theory of Employment, Interest and Money: The Collected Writings of John Maynard Keynes*, vol. VII. London: Royal Economic Society and Cambridge University Press.

9

MONEY EXPLAINED

Liquidity Preference and the Interest Rate

A small recap of our discussion might help organize the ideas of *The General Theory* unpacked so far. Effective demand is the main determinant of Keynes' theory of production because it explains employment. But what defines effective demand? Keynes answered this question by exploring the determinants of each component of effective demand. Consumption is determined by income, whereas the propensity to consume sets the amount of income that individuals consume. The other component of effective demand in *The General Theory* is investment, the determinants of which are the marginal efficiency of capital, which was explained in the last chapter, and the interest rate, which we now investigate.

We explore what the interest rate is and how its value is defined in the financial markets. Another important concept of *The General Theory* that emerges alongside interest is liquidity preference. It is worth noting that, if we are talking about the interest rate, our conversation necessarily involves money. In our presentation of *The General Theory* until now, money has appeared from time to time, but in a somewhat incidental manner. From this point, however, money occupies its due place as a protagonist of *The General Theory*, in which Keynes delivered his picture of capitalism as a monetary economy of production. As the name, monetary economy of production, suggests, money and production are intertwined in the economy. Although money can affect production via consumption, it is through investment that the entanglement of money and production occurs. This is because of the role the interest rate plays in determining investment. This chapter and the next unravel this thread.

Liquidity Preference and the Interest Rate

When a person receives income, she makes two decisions. The first is about how much she wants to consume, a choice that depends on her propensity to consume.

DOI: 10.4324/9781003287094-13

The second decision is related to the first, but it concerns that part of her income which remains following her consumption decision, namely, her savings. After segregating the bulk of her income for consumption, she is left with her savings in hand, and then she needs to decide the asset she will use to store those savings. Would it be money? Bitcoin? Gold? Public bonds? Shares? Capital goods, such as a machine to produce ice-cream? The answer to this question depends on the very important concept formulated by Keynes in *The General Theory*, liquidity preference.

Earlier, we explained that liquidity refers to how easily an asset can be converted to money. But why is money the benchmark? Because it is the most liquid asset in the economy. As such, money can, at any time, liquidate any economic transactions, for example, settling debts or buying goods, services, houses, capital goods, or financial assets. No asset, other than money, has such liquidity. Therefore, assets that are quickly, easily, and cheaply turned back into money, like some saving deposits, public bonds, or shares, are more liquid. By contrast, the more distant assets are from being quickly, easily, and cheaply exchanged for money, the less liquid they are. Thus, capital goods, for example, are normally extremely illiquid. Put simply, the closer to money a person's assets are, the more liquid she is. The farther her assets are from being convertible to money, the more illiquid she becomes.

Observe that there is a gradation of liquidity in the economy; it is measured by comparing the extent to which an asset is distant from the fully liquid asset, money. Considered in this way, when deciding how to keep her savings, liquidity preference is how willing a person is for her savings to take a form closer or farther from money. Therefore, the liquidity preference of individuals ranges between different degrees. For each grade of liquidity preference, a particular asset class will be chosen.

A given preference is a personal and subjective position that emerges from individual expectations. If circumstances shift, uncertainty changes and ensues new expectations. Accordingly, individuals modify their preferences for one asset or another based on their liquidity. When people hold money in hand or in a checking account, they are expressing their preference for the greatest liquidity. If they decrease their desire for liquidity, they exchange their cash for other less liquid assets. Hence, people's aggregate liquidity preference translates itself into the demand for money in the economy.

This does not mean, however, that all individuals have the same preference for liquidity. The diversity of expectations, and consequently of opinions, guarantees individuals prefer different liquidities. The only time this is not the case is the rare situation, that happens only during severe crises, of the liquidity trap. In such crises, uncertainty becomes so extreme that the convention prevailing in the community is of such a bad future that the liquidity preference becomes absolute. As a result, people retain no other asset than money or, at the most, checking accounts with banks. Individuals thus understand money as a safe economic thing that preserves value in its most liquid form; therefore, when making decisions, it is toward money that people direct their dearest consideration.

What then is the interest rate? Remember that individuals make two decisions about how they use their income. First, their propensity to consume determines how much they consume out of income. Their second decision concerns how to hold the saved share of income. If a person leaves her savings in money, she has an absolute preference for liquidity. If she has a lower preference for liquidity, she agrees to forego the liquidity that money offers. What does she gain in doing so? The answer is the interest rate.

Interest is the reward individuals receive when they consent to cede their liquidity for a time period. Individuals forgoing the full liquidity of money incur in a series of risks, for which the compensation is the interest rate they expect to gain in respect of the assets they exchanged their money for. Hence, the interest rate measures the willingness of people to take on the risks of giving up their liquidity. It is thus the reward for not hoarding money or the return individuals gain for lending to borrowers the security of liquidity. In other, rather technical words, the interest rate is the premium paid to those investors who decide to face immeasurable uncertainty by parting with the liquidity of their money to buy debts from borrowers in the financial markets.

We saw earlier that, in comparison to Keynes' approach, neoclassical economics considers the interest rate as the price of not consuming today and waiting for the future to do so. Individuals who save will consume more in the future by adding to their income the interest obtained from lending their savings in the loanable funds market. As such, the interest rate is the price of parsimony. The thriftier people are in the present, the greater their consumption in the future. In aggregate, interest rates are the price that balances the demand for, and supply of, loanable funds.

However, as Keynes explained, if money itself is saved, there is no interest rate obtained. Thus, there is no such thing as interest rates being the reward that compensates thrifty investors who wait for the future to consume. Interest rates do not reward waiting. They reward the unsafe action of investors parting with their liquidity to plow money into risky debts sold by risky borrowers in the financial markets. Therefore, interest rates are not the prize for saving. They are the prize for confronting the never perfectly measurable uncertainty with which people must engage when they invest what were once liquid savings.

Rather than its general and abstract concept, what we really know about the interest rate is the number it assumes and according to which people either discharge or gain some amount of money. How is this rate, this number, this value defined? Keynes explained this in *The General Theory* by setting out a simple scheme synthesizing the factors that motivate individuals and firms to demand money. He called these the psychological and business incentives to liquidity, though he could as well have titled them the psychological and business preferences for liquidity.

The Motives for Demanding Money and the Determinacy of Interest Rates

In his schematic presentation in *The General Theory*, Keynes advanced three main reasons individuals and firms demand money. These are the transactions motive, the precautionary motive, and the speculative motive. All are important, but it is the third – the speculative motive – that matters most to the definition of interest rates. Let us explore each of these reasons grounding money demand.

Keynes divided the transactions motive into the income motive of individuals and the business motive of firms. However, the logic underlying these two motives is the same. The transactions motive is the demand for money for individuals, families, and businesses to meet their day-to-day needs. In general, rents received do not perfectly match the expenditures that everyday life demands. Underlying this motive is that individuals, families, and firms use money as a means of exchange. It is the response to the first question individuals ask on receiving income, how much should I hold for consumption? If income, like workers' wages or firms' proceeds, provides the funds for consumption, it also determines money demand for transactions – it would be impossible for anyone to afford spending indefinitely without a regular source of income.

From this motive, Keynes formulated the notion of the income velocity of money. It is the speed at which a unit of money circulates due to the transactions motive. Since the economy's aggregate income and consumption pattern do not change abruptly, the propensity to consume, the transactions motive, and the income velocity of money are reasonably stable in the short run. In the long term, however, changes in factors such as habits, income distribution, banking organization, and technology change the income velocity of money. For instance, the technological advancement, the current apex of which is virtual wallets and digital national currencies, has made it easier and thus faster for a unit of money to circulate. This has increased the speed at which a unit of money moves around and has reduced the amount of money retained for transactions.

The second reason for demanding money is the precautionary motive. This is the holding of money as a reserve of value to confront contingencies or to take advantage of profitable transaction opportunities. Uncertainty is the reason behind the existence of this motive. Since the future is unknowable, people might prefer to hoard money because it allows them the freedom to face unexpected events, whether bad or good. Income also determines the precautionary motive, much as it does define the transactions motive: it is impossible to engage in precautionary saving without a regular source of income. Nevertheless, with a given income, ease of access to credit and the level of interest rates influences the amount of money held for both motives.

The precautionary motive emphasizes the role of money as a value reserve. Money is an asset; therefore, it is wealth. But, unlike other assets, money maintains the holder's wealth with huge value stability and the greatest liquidity in the economy. The absolute liquidity preference of individuals is, in fact, their share of precautionary money demand. In this sense, any investment by individuals, or even any big expenditure that people make, like buying a house, is a departure from this safe place of having money in hand as precaution. Carvalho (2015) called this logic defensive behavior, and it has overwhelming dominance over people's relationship with money; their first thought about the form their savings should take is not about which asset to invest in, but about how dangerous it is to depart from holding money. In this approach, the interest rate is the price that compensates savers who are bold enough to make financial investments and take the risks of ceding their liquidity.

The third reason to demand money is the speculative motive. Keynes defined this as demanding money for "the objective of securing profit from knowing better than the market what the future will bring forth" (2013d, p. 170). This definition by Keynes may suggest that one or a few individuals can decipher the future. However, this is not the correct interpretation. Those who better read the future only make a better wager than other investors about the future performance of financial assets. So, driven by the speculative motive, individuals demand money and use it in financial investments in an attempt to make more money. When individuals purchase securities, public bonds, crypto-assets, or shares, and when they make savings deposits at banks, they are following their speculative motive. They are trying to make more money with the money they invested.

In this sense, the speculative demand for money is a kind of bridge connecting the individual demand for money for speculative purposes and the individual supply of this same money to the financial markets. For instance, depositing in a savings account means that the account holder exchanged money for an asset. While they first held money as an asset, they then used it to buy another asset. They demanded money first and then supplied it to banks in the financial market in exchange for the asset they purchased. The same reasoning is true for the purchase of other assets, like securities and public bonds. Hence, the buying of a financial asset for speculative purposes is an act that supplies money to the financial market. However, this money supply is only generated after individuals demand money out of their income to satisfy the speculative motive.

This supply of money to the financial market also implies individuals relinquishing the full liquidity of money. Why would they do this? Their rationale is to receive the interest rate, which is the price of negotiating the full liquidity of money. These movements involving either supplying money in exchange for assets or selling assets to demand money for precautionary purposes define the interest rate. Investors enter the financial market, while others leave as a result of differences in expectations. These differences ensure various degrees of liquidity preference among individuals. Accordingly, money supply and demand, and thus interest rates, change. Keeping all other variables constant, in each market of the financial system, money supply greater than money demand reduces the interest rate, and money demand bigger than money supply elevates the interest rate.

Some examples might help illustrate these movements. A higher liquidity preference because of negative expectations of the future, causes people to demand money for precautionary reasons. These individuals will not return their money to the financial system soon, thereby the supply of money reduces and this pushes interest rates up. By contrast, if expectations of gains arise and lower individuals' liquidity preference, there will be more investment in financial assets, causing an increase in the supply of money and a consequent interest rate decrease. Moreover, if people in the market are only willing to change assets in their portfolio, money demand for speculative motives and its supply to the financial market will not change. The difference is that in this case, money will be withdrawn from those specific assets deemed riskier by investors, and, in turn, assets evaluated as safer will be purchased. Consequently, markets in which investments are withdrawn see rising interest rates, and the ones that receive this flow of investment notice interest rates going down. This movement suggests an overall higher degree of liquidity preference that excludes specific assets that might otherwise be bought. Still, this higher liquidity preference is not as strong as it needs to be to reduce the liquidity in the financial system overall.

In *The General Theory*, Keynes recalled the labels he advanced in *A Treatise on Money* to describe the two behaviors dominating the financial markets, those of bear and bull. The former has positive expectations of markets and a lower liquidity preference. They expect to profit by speculatively demanding money to buy financial assets. Bear agents reason the other way round. Expecting a worsening future, they are driven by their liquidity preference to sell assets and carry money instead. Individuals are distributed between these two behaviors, and the confrontations between bear and bull agents explain the daily fluctuations of interest rates. The normal discrepancies between these two groups are not sufficiently strong to cause extreme disturbances in the financial market. Major disturbances may happen, and although they happen less often, they are neither uncommon. When such disturbances occur, they set off rapid and remarkable downward or upward trends in the market, leading the system to experience a crisis or a boom, respectively.

In light of these behaviors and their impacts, Keynes concluded that the interest rate is a conventional phenomenon. It is a midpoint that results from the countless expectations driving different degrees of liquidity preference in the financial markets. These expectations and liquidity preferences converge into two big groups, bears and bulls, that represent two major conventions, bulls awaiting markets in ascension and bears anticipating losses. The market will be in between these two conventions; thus, the interest rate is a conventional element emerging from the confront between different conventions concerning the likely path the market will take.

Whereas income explains the transactions and precautionary motive for money demand, the interest rate explains the speculative motive. More precisely, what explains the speculative reason for demanding money is the expected variation of the interest rate over time. The variation of interest rates causes changes in the market prices of assets, implying gains or losses for those who hold them. Thus, these asset bearers must form expectations about how they hope market prices will behave. Different liquidity preferences thus emerge, and money supply and demand in the financial market float accordingly.

Nevertheless, the shape of expectations concerning the future path of interest rates does not only account for the specific performance of a particular asset. Individuals form expectations by gathering all available information about the asset itself and about other assets and macroeconomic variables such as inflation, GDP, and the exchange rate. All these elements contribute to the formation of expectations about how interest rates might change from the current moment, when the asset is purchased, to the future. This expected variation, in turn, determines the speculative motive for demanding money and forms the interest rate.

In this sense, different from the transactions motive, whose stability over time is remarkable, the speculative motive can shift as rapidly as expectations change, and this makes liquidity preferences vary. Financial crises, as well as booming periods, result from this buoyant nature of expectations, which can cause fast points of inflection from the latter to the former occur, as is exemplified by the 2008 sub-prime crisis. The precautionary motive shifts fast, too. In moments of crisis, where the speculative money demand decreases, money is held as a precaution. With a boom, the inverse is expected; the speculative motive tends to grow, reducing the hoarding of money.

Incidentally, the assets in the financial system have yield expressed in forms other than just interest. Shares or crypto-assets, for example, do not pay interest. Individuals buy these assets pursuing to profit through the variation in their price – those who purchase shares may also intend to earn dividends from the companies whose shares they own. Still, the logic underlying the speculative motive continues to be true. Financial investors are always wagering that they will be on the right side of price and/or interest rate variations. The focus Keynes gave to the interest rate is because it is the most important return rate in the financial system. Those deciding whether or not to invest and in what to invest first look to interest rates. Hence, movements in the price of both shares and crypto-assets can happen as responses to changes in the interest rate, such is its importance to the economy. This explains why the interest rate is one of the variables determining productive investments.

Since the 2010s, some central banks have been setting zero or even negative interest rates. When central banks mark their interest rates, they are trying to influence the direction of market rates. However, Keynes argued, the rates autonomously set in the market, which are those negotiated by bear and bull agents, without central banks being part of the transaction, cannot reach this terrain of zero or negative lower bound. Unlike the rates of central banks, the lower bound of nominal market rates is positive (the real interest rate can be negative, but this is because of inflation and not due to agents setting negative nominal interest rates to buy other people's debt). Notwithstanding being this floor positive, the lower the market rate, the riskier individuals judge markets as being and the higher their liquidity preference becomes.

But why is this the case? First, Keynes explained, several other risks are taken into account in establishing an interest rate. Central banks can fairly neglect these risks given their power to issue money, but this is impossible for all other market agents. Keynes enumerated a few risks that enter the calculus of market agents, such as the risk of wrong expectations, moral hazard, liquidity, and inflation. All these risks contribute to forming the market rate of interest and thus to keeping it positive.

Second, a too-low interest rate does not meet the conventional or habitual interest rate that spurs individuals to buy financial assets. In *A Treatise on Money*, Wicksellian Keynes called this rate the natural interest rate. In *The General Theory*,

Keynes changed his mind and stated that the interest rate that motivates people to lean into the financial markets is not natural but conventional, shaped by individual habits and expectations. As such, a too-low interest rate discourages people from investing in the financial system because it does not pay the minimum interest rate their individual habits stipulate as the appropriate compensation for the risks of parting with their liquidity.

Third, when the interest rate is at a low level, small changes in the rate cause variations greater than those happening at higher rates. Then, even small changes in low interest rates can result in considerable shifts in market conditions. For instance, an interest rate increase from 1% to 2% is a variation of 100%. A change in the interest rate from 4% to 5% is a variation of 25%. Finally, a rate increasing from 10% to 11% is only a 10% change. The point here is that the lower the interest rate gets, the greater the impact on asset prices when it varies; accordingly, agents assess the market as riskier. Because of this, central banks have a hard time ensuring soft landings in the economy after they enact expansionary monetary policies involving lowering their interest rates. A word of caution is needed, though. Even with the concerns about the impacts of low interest rates, Keynes suggested that, whenever the circumstances allow, central banks should manage their interest rates to the lowest levels to avoid the effects of high interest rates on investment.

These three factors set a positive limit to the market interest rate. In addition, the longer the debt contract, the higher the interest rate. Thus, the yield curve or the term structure of the interest rate, which is the line connecting all interest rates negotiated in the market to different time periods, is an ascendant curve. The level of interest rates that form the yield curve depends on how long the debt contract lasts. The longer the term, the higher the interest rate and, in turn, the yield curve. There can be other inclinations in the yield curve, but they are transitory and usually indicate that market agents outlook changes in the circumstances.

In the final part of the previous chapter, we saw that the marginal efficiency of capital, the other determinant of investment, decreases over time. Thus, there is a cross-road investments reach in the long term. While the marginal efficiency of capital, which is the rate of return of capital goods, reduces as aggregate investment increases, interest rates not only have a lower positive limit, but they also surge upward the longer the term of the debt contract. Notwithstanding the fact that the marginal efficiency of capital is overly dependent on subjective elements like expectations, state of confidence, and animal spirits, and it is also decrescent over time, investment is as well affected by the always positive and increasing term structure of the interest rate. Investments are, thus, a fragile thing; nevertheless, employment and production depend on them.

Three Further Considerations on the Determinacy of Investment

The two determinants of aggregate demand's most important component, investment, are the marginal efficiency of capital and the interest rate. These two rates of return are an alternative to each other. Hence, they compete as means through which wealth owners can plow money into when they try to become wealthier. A marginal efficiency of capital greater than the interest rate that financial assets pay causes wealth owners to invest productively. By contrast, if the interest rate is greater than the marginal efficiency of capital, it discourages the purchase of capital goods. Consequently, the interest rate sets the limit to investments entrepreneurs agree to make. Accordingly, it also establishes the limits of employment and GDP growth.

In light of that, there are three further considerations we need to make regarding the determinacy of investment by the marginal efficiency of capital and the interest rate. First, these two variables are independent of each other. The return given by the interest rate has no primary relation to the expected prospective yields and the investment cost that shapes the marginal efficiency of capital. Likewise, these two variables that form the marginal efficiency of capital do not set the interest rate. As a result of the independence between the marginal efficiency of capital and the interest rate, movements in one do not directly cause movements in the other.

A lower interest rate does not necessarily and automatically cause a greater marginal efficiency of capital, and vice versa. The effects of one of these variables can reach the other, but through their determinacy on other variables such as investment, consumption, or demand for credit. For instance, a higher interest rate can reduce the prospective yields that entrepreneurs expect to gain, or it can increase the investment cost by elevating the cost of funding investment plans; through these indirect ways, it can reach and depress the marginal efficiency of capital. Or a strong scale of investments pushed by an exciting marginal efficiency of capital can increase the demand for funds in the financial market, pushing the interest rate up. Nevertheless, this is not the same thing as the variations of the interest rate being the primary, direct cause of the shifts of the marginal efficiency of capital or the other way round.

Second, readers, please do not bear in mind any automatic or hydraulic reasoning when you think in Keynesian terms. Let us remind you that Keynes was the economist who brought uncertainty to economics. Since expectations matter, a lower interest rate will not automatically lift productive investment just as a higher interest rate is not an automatic locker of investments. Keynes did not reason hydraulically in *The General Theory*. The hydraulic view of Keynes emerged when John Hicks brought about his IS-LM model, later known as the Keynesian model. Hick's model was written in a mathematical language that presets the relationship between the variables. A variable necessarily reacts to its determinant in only one direction. Investment was positively determined by income and negatively by the interest rate. Thus, the hydraulic reasoning: a falling interest rate must be accompanied by increasing investment. This model has been taught worldwide as if it were Keynesian theory. But Hicks was not Keynes, and his theory was not actually Keynesian theory.

In Keynes' theory, in normal circumstances, a low interest rate has the effect of not being another variable encumbering the hard choice which is to make a productive investment. Therefore, greater investment usually, but not necessarily accompanies a low interest rate. However, expectations of poor prospective yields or a distrustful state of confidence in the calculus of future profits can discourage investment even in the presence of falling or low interest rates. In crises, central banks settle their interest rates down to avoid making them one further factor hindering investments. Nevertheless, this is a bid of central banks. There is no certainty that the crisis ravaging the economy will stop and recovery will begin just because the central bank's interest rate is low. If any hydraulic economic reasoning were to be true, why has the world seen so many economic and social crises happening over time?

Third, expectations determine both the prospective yields of the marginal efficiency of capital and the interest rate. Entrepreneurs calculate the marginal efficiency of capital's prospective yields based on long-term expectations about the future conditions of the real economy. Expectations about the variation of interest rates determine degrees of liquidity preferences and these set the demand for, and supply of, money in the financial markets, thereby defining interest rates. In this sense, given the defensive behavior of individuals that we talked about earlier, we can say that a productive investment is made after the expectations of individuals have driven them to surpass two defensive desires, first, for holding money, and second for investing in financial assets.

Let us translate this reasoning to the monetary economy of production, which is Keynes' concept of capitalism. The capital movement of *capital*ism is wealth production and accumulation. This process necessarily requires the possession of cash, which is a form of wealth. But if individuals just hoard money, they cannot gain more money to augment their wealth. Therefore, individuals must forego the safety of money if they pursue to become richier. Hence, individuals have two options which, obviously, are the determinants of productive investment, the variable that Keynes needed to scrutinize in order to theorize the general theory of employment within the monetary economy of production.

On the one hand, if individuals prefer liquidity, they lay out their money in financial assets looking to earn interest. Consequently, the aggregate investment in the economy reduces or, at best, remains the same. On the other hand, given a good state of confidence of individuals, they might not fall for the liquidity fetish if they calculate, based on their long-term expectations, a marginal efficiency of capital sufficient to make them buy illiquid capital assets. This latter case means productive investment. It drives Keynes' demand-led economics and explains the creation of jobs, production, income, and wealth.

Decisions toward buying capital goods are the last step individuals take when they are deciding by which means they will try to increase their wealth. Holding money is the first stage at which individuals can place themselves. But it means an absolute liquidity preference from which no more money can be earned. The gain of interest in the financial market is the second stage individuals can go to. The decision in favor of making a productive investment is, in this sense, the third possible and outmost step. It is the choice that places individuals at the most distant from money and thus illiquid and unsafe assets, which are also the most submissive to the passage of time among all assets in the economy. Nevertheless, it is the most important economic choice in capitalism.

Money, through the interest rate, plays a role in making investments fragile. But why is this the case for money and not for other assets? Has money got any special characteristics when compared with financial assets or capital goods? The answer is yes; money has peculiarities. The next chapter reveals and explains these, and thereby it discloses *money*, the remaining piece of the puzzle called *The General Theory of Employment, Interest and Money*.

References

Carvalho, F. J. C. (2015). 'Keynes on Expectations, Uncertainty and Defensive Behavior', *Brazilian Keynesian Review*, 1(1), pp. 44–54.

Keynes, J. M. (2013b). *A Treatise on Money I, the Pure Theory of Money: The Collected Writings of John Maynard Keynes*, vol. V. London: Cambridge University Press.

Keynes, J. M. (2013c). *A Treatise on Money II, the Applied Theory of Money: The Collected Writings of John Maynard Keynes*, vol. VI. London: Cambridge University Press.

Keynes, J. M. (2013d). *The General Theory of Employment, Interest and Money: The Collected Writings of John Maynard Keynes*, vol. VII. London: Royal Economic Society and Cambridge University Press.

10

MONEY EXPLAINED

Why Is It so Special in the Economy?
The Peculiarities of Money

By the end of the last chapter, we emphasized that it is the interest rate on money that matters most to the economy. It sets the limit on the expansion of investment, employment, and production. We also said that money is an asset unlike all other assets because it is pure liquidity; in fact, it benchmarks the liquidity of all other financial and capital assets. It is around money that the liquidity preferences of individuals gravitate. People only choose options other than money when their animal spirits thrust them to think that making illiquid choices, like buying capital goods will enable them to profit by producing goods and services. Otherwise, uncertainty can cause individuals to prefer greater liquidity, pushing them to purchase assets that can quickly and easily be converted to money. In both cases, money is the gravitational center from which individuals' economic choices depart but which they are always ready to return, for either safety or profit realization.

This flow away and back to money is not neutral to the economy. A decision to hold money is a decision neither to hold capital goods nor to employ workers to operate them. In that event, production does not increase as it would do if money had been spent acquiring capital goods, employing workers, or starting or expanding production. Money thus affects economic activity: it hinders the production of goods and services and determines how many workers are employed. Therefore, the interest rate, which is the price of money, is another important economic variable. If individuals are to part with their money and make investments (either financial or productive), the interest rate on money is the lower limit that all other assets must pay in order to be acquired.

But why is money this special thing? What has it got that no other asset in the economy has? Why is money the center of gravity around which the economic system orbits? Is there any other such gravitational center besides money? This chapter explores the discussion about money, and with it, the theoretical content of *The General Theory* finishes as well. The comprehension of the special characteristics of

DOI: 10.4324/9781003287094-14

money, which make it such a special asset in the economy, furnishes the last piece of *The General Theory's* puzzle.

The Asset Price Theory

To explain the idiosyncrasies of money, Keynes advanced an asset pricing theory. Every asset in the economy has a return, which can be measured by balancing four variables. The first is the return on the asset, which we shall call q. The second is capital gain or loss, which is the variation of the asset's value over time. In fact, Keynes did not input this variable in the formula he presented in Chapter 17 of *The General Theory*. He talked about it just after presenting the formula and explained that it would add gains, if the asset's value rises, or subtract losses, if the asset's value drops, from the total return of the asset. Let us designate it a, as Keynes did, and insert it direct in the formula, different from what Keynes did, but this does not change his theory. The third is the asset's liquidity premium, l. The closer to money the asset is, the greater its liquidity premium is. Capital assets have a negligible liquidity premium, financial assets have some (the extent of which depends on the degree of development of their secondary markets), and money has the maximum liquidity premium. The final component of the equation is the cost of carrying financial assets or using capital goods, which Keynes labeled c. As with any cost, c is negative in the formula. Take q, a, l, and c, and the return on any asset is as follows:

$$Return = q \pm a + l - c.$$

Financial assets can have fixed income q, but they are liable to market-to-market price variations of their face value a; if they have well-developed secondary markets, their l is good and low c. Financial assets like common shares can also have a variable income. Common shares have good l and low c but do not pay q. Their stockholders hope to gain a. Bearers of crypto-assets are in the same position as common shares' holders; they want to profit from a good positive variation of a. The difference is that stock markets have well-developed secondary markets that, apart from a few, crypto-assets mostly have not got, so their l is very low. Some crypto-assets also have an expensive carrying and/or mining cost. Holders of crypto-assets therefore face great risks when they seek to profit from a rising a. Entrepreneurs, such as the ice-cream maker of our example, buy capital goods on account of the high q they expect. Within capital goods, a is as a negligible source of return as l, and they have, on average, a reasonable cost of use c.

In turn, money has neither q, a, nor c (c is only relevant during hyperinflation). But money has full l. This is the return on money: unrestricted liquidity, representing and offering safety against uncertainty. In so far as uncertainty is an unavoidable feature of every economic decision, no one never dismisses the return in terms of safety that money's full liquidity yields. On the contrary, individuals prize it; in crises, it is the most valuable return that can be had.

At the end of Chapter 8, when discussing the marginal efficiency of capital, we said that the return on capital goods reduces as the stock of investments increases. One reason for this decreasing marginal efficiency of capital is scarcity. A capital asset X, like a machine to prepare ice-cream, whose q is better than other assets, will be in demand by entrepreneurs. But as the scarcity of X reduces, so does its expected return q. If a city has a great number of ice-creamers, the price of each ice-cream will fall. A similar reasoning holds for financial assets. The scarcity of lenders parting with their liquidity to buy a certain debt, pushes up the interest charged on it. An abundance of lenders supplying their money in the financial markets works contrariwise and brings down market interest rates.

In this sense, the asset whose return is steadiest, or at least diminishes at the slowest pace, is the one that sets the limit of return for all the other assets in the economy. If the world had no uncertainty, individuals would fearlessly jump from one asset to another, according to the relative scarcity between them. When agents' risk-free movements balance the relative scarcity of all assets, their return would become the same. However, there is no such world ruled over by certainty. In the actual world of monetary economies of production, uncertainty is unavoidable. Returns are a bet made by individuals, not a sure thing. Consequently, uncertainty also invokes fear, or, in rather more Keynesian words, liquidity preference.

To reiterate: the asset with the steadiest return is the one most prized in the economy, and the one on which individuals focus. This asset is money – which should not come as a surprise, given the attention we have been paying to it and the things we have been saying about it! The mystery here is not that money is the star of the monetary economy of production. The mystery is, *why* is it the star?

The Peculiarities of Money

The answer is that money is a special asset because of three peculiarities. First, the elasticity of production of money is negligible or close to zero. This hard-to-understand sentence has an easy-to-comprehend meaning. Elasticity is the response that a cause-variable implies in an effect-variable. Take the purchasing power of money (or as Keynes said, the price of money) as the cause-variable and the supply of money as the effect-variable. When the exchange value of money rises, that is, when its purchase power increases, the production of money does not follow suit, because money cannot be freely produced. If you try to print American Dollars or Brazilian Reals, dear reader, you are likely to go to jail for money counterfeiting. Businesspeople cannot employ workers to produce money if its purchasing power increases as they can do when the price of what they produce goes up and offers them a greater return.

This first postulate means that money is deliberately scarce in the economy. Central banks are responsible for preserving money scarcity: not for nothing are they countries' monetary authorities. Central banks are not the only supplier of money in the economy, but banks also supply money. In countries with well-developed financial systems, banks supply most of money; still, they do so with the clearance, and under the strict surveillance, of central banks. Monetary policy is the name of the job through which central banks take care of a country's currency; the supply of money is therefore under constant and active vigilance. However, money management does not signify that central banks fully control money supply; the banking system creates money and central banks do not tabulate the volume of money that banks will create. Equally, this absence of full control does not mean that central banks should do nothing to supervise money supply. Since his 1923 *A Tract*, Keynes continuously asked for monetary management. He believed that central banks must try to influence and direct, as much as possible, the banking system's money creation.

Some other assets in the economy, like gold or even some financial assets, are also not produced at will; why are they not money? Money has a second idiosyncratic attribute: its elasticity of substitution is also negligible or zero. Remember that elasticity is the response that one variable causes in another variable; then, elasticity of substitution is how money demand responds to changes in its purchasing power (or in its exchange value). The utility of money lies in it being an asset whose pure liquidity guarantees a continue exchange value in either spot or future transactions. Money is thus the ultimate value reserve because, in normal conditions, anyone who has money can liquidate any transaction at any time. This is the purest form of wealth's power to command everything in the economy. Hence, in normal circumstances, money is not substituted for any other asset if its purchasing power changes. Consequently, the demand for money remains stable.

Please do not misunderstand us here: *stable demand* does not mean that a desire for $10 now will be followed by a desire for $10 tomorrow and the same $10 next month, next year, or next century. Stable demand has a more general meaning, signifying that the country's currency, like the Dollar in the USA, the Euro in the Euro Zone, Real in Brazil, or the Rand in South Africa, is the subject of continuous demand. So, the gist of the stable demand for money, which emerges from its very small or negligible elasticity of substitution, is not the ongoing demand for the $10, but the hourly demand for the currency $, irrespective of the bigger or smaller number that this demand for $, i.e., for money, assumes over time.

Together, these two elasticities mean that the currency of the country is always in demand; however, the supply of money ensures that it is kept scarce relative to the demand for it. The balance struck between people always demanding money and central banks managing its supply grants money a stable value. This stable value, in turn, convinces individuals to use the country's money not only as means of exchange in spot transactions but also (and especially) as a value reserve in which to store wealth. Being socially valued by individuals, money is always accepted in whatever transactions people engage; this is, in practice, the demonstration of its full liquidity.

Central banks are responsible for managing the supply of money relatively to the demand for it in the economy. Thus, monetary authorities play a special role in maintaining people's belief in the credibility of a certain currency. The importance of credibility is related to money's status as a convention. The people of a country do not take it for granted but must believe in the national currency as something deserving of their ready confidence. After all, money is wealth, and who would store wealth in an untrustworthy asset? Central banks generate social confidence in the currency by managing money's elasticity of production in relation to the demand for it. So, they back money as the convention to which people entrust their wealth. Central banks are the key players behind the use of money as a special asset in the economy, around which the economic system rotates.

This is a somewhat abstract view of how money operates in the economy. But this is because money is such a peculiar creature that we can say that it breaks the law of logic and is, at the same time, a concrete abstract element (well, we know that might sound a contradiction in terms, but not in the case of money). Throughout history, different societies have used various things to be money. Gold, silver, copper, salt, and shells have all been used to pay debts and settle spot and forward transactions. These were all money. Even the scapegoat, an animal released into the wilderness to atone for human sins, was a kind of money used to settle divine debts.

In each society, a dominant entity whose power people recognize and obey, like the king, the State, the church, or the shaman, can select something to be the community's money. The hourly usage of this currency, though, only remains in place if people trust that this currency permits the maintenance of their wealth. If people mistrust the country's money for whatever reason, they will either reject its use or, at best, hold only the amount needed to settle a few everyday transactions, like buying food or paying taxes. The rest of their wealth they would store in other assets that they believed would better preserve their reserves.

Modern money is chartalist, meaning that national States have the power to choose their country's currency; yet the life and success of the currency depend on people's confidence in it. It is the shared confidence of individuals in a currency that creates the convention that makes this currency the country's currency over time. Brazil's history offers interesting examples that show how money is a convention that totally depends on people's confidence in it.

In the 1980s, Brazil suffered hyperinflation and the economic authorities substituted the country's currency for a new one whenever the accumulated inflation became intolerable. In January 1989, in an effort to quell inflation, Brazil launched Cruzado Novo, its third currency in five years. As a new currency, the Cruzado Novo was devoid of accumulated inflation. Some inflation from the recent past may have caused some price variation when the Cruzado Novo was first introduced, but not enough to make people reject it due to high inflation deteriorating its purchasing power. Nevertheless, rejection occurred.

Brazilians mistrusted the economic authorities so deeply that they found it impossible to have confidence in the new currency as a store of wealth. They refused to use the new money: as soon as they received payments in Cruzado Novo, they exchanged it for any other thing they believed was more valuable or more reliable than the new currency. As people abandoned the Cruzado Novo exchanging it for other things, the velocity of its circulation increased meaning that its elasticity of substitution did not remain zero or at least small. Inflation soared, fueled by the rapidity with which Brazilians exchanged every Cruzado Novo note and coin for other goods and assets. It became a shared belief, that is, a convention, that the new currency did not deserve to be trusted. By March 1990, the government has to discontinue the Cruzado Novo and instead adopt yet another new currency, Cruzeiro, the fourth in six years.

Brazil also had an interesting monetary experience in the opposite direction. In 1994, the country got rid of hyperinflation with the Real Plan. This plan created a monetary system with two currencies, the Cruzeiro Real and the Real Unit of Value (the *Unidade Real de Valor*, better known by its acronym, URV). The first currency was a unit of account as well as the only means of exchange in the country. The second was *only* a unit of account, used to denominate wages, taxes, public utility bills, bank account balances, and so on. Moreover, there was a monetary rate of conversion between the two national currencies as well as between the URV and the US Dollar.

The government corrected and announced the equivalence between the two national currencies daily but cleverly kept the value of URV at 1, while this 1 was equivalent to a bigger amount of Cruzeiro Reais every day. The URV was launched on March 1, 1994, and thereafter individuals saw, every day, 1 URV valuing more and more in terms of Cruzeiro Reais. On the URV's first day, it was equal to 647.50 Cruzeiro Reais. One month later, 1 URV was equal to 931.05 Cruzeiro Reais. After two months, 1 URV equaled 1,323.92 Cruzeiro Reais. Finally, on June 30, 1994, the last day of the bi-monetary system, 1 URV was valued at 2,750.00 Cruzeiro Reais. The value of the URV in terms of US Dollars was also kept at 1. However, because the Cruzeiro Real was the sole means of exchange, the parity between the URV and the Dollar was nothing more than a statement. If individuals wanted to buy US Dollars, they had to do so using Cruzeiro Reais.

The Cruzeiro Real was the only means of exchange and was the currency used to purchase goods and services and repay debts. Prices in the economy rose only in Cruzeiro Reais. For four months, from March to June 1994, Brazilians noticed the URV maintaining its value at 1, and 1 was also the URV/US Dollar parity. At the same time, they saw the Cruzeiro Real losing its exchange value in relation to goods, services, the URV, and the US Dollar. Yet during this period, the URV could not be used; it existed as a unit of account only. Without circulating, its elasticity of production was absolutely zero.

Individuals, however, *wanted* to use the URV. They could see for themselves the stability of its value. During the four months of Brazil's dual currency, people's confidence in the URV grew. They knew it would eventually become the country's sole currency, but nobody, not even the government, acknowledged beforehand when. This was an incredibly smart strategy. These four months were needed to make people trust in the URV. As the months went by, people's confidence in the URV grew, as did the belief that it would be a sound and stable new currency. This, of course, only served to increase the demand for it further. On July 1, 1994, the URV became the Real, the successful currency still used today in Brazil.

These histories tell us that money is a convention, and successful conventions are expressions of social confidence. The confidence that supports people's use of money does not fall like manna from heaven. It does not even come only from the power of the State itself. It relies on reflexivity between State and society. This means that money as a convention depends on central banks reliably managing money's elasticity of supply in relation to the demand for it. Objective and subjective factors can change liquidity preference and, in turn, the demand for money. Central banks respond to these changes by both taking action directly in their monetary policies and overviewing the behavior of the banking and financial systems.

Last, but not least, the scarcity of money for which Keynes advocated did not refer to a certain absolute amount of money supply, as is the case of the quantity theory of money and the theories it inspired, such as neoclassical economics. Keynes' idea was that the elasticity of production is relative to the demand for money. In crises, for example, when the liquidity preference grows rapidly and intensely, the supply of money must follow suit. In these cases, individuals are so afraid of the future that they hold all money they can. If the supply of money increases, individuals can be convinced that money, their object of desire, is easily accessible, softening their desire for hoarding it and its consequences for effective demand. In booms, when liquidity preference decreases, central banks elevate interest rates and reduce money supply, in an attempt to dissuade individuals from intensely changing money for other assets in the real economy.

However, the theories inspired by the quantity theory of money state that the currency in circulation must be the exact number that results from the ratio between the monetary value of the GDP (the aggregate price times the GDP) and money velocity of circulation. For instance, in numerical parlance, say, if prices are 2, GDP is 10, and a unit of money circulates at speed 4, the supply of money must be $\frac{(2*10)}{4}$, that is, 5. If it is greater than that, inflation surges; if less, deflation emerges.

Besides the two peculiar elasticities, there is a third peculiarity, which consists of a group of factors that combine to make money a special asset in the economy. First, prices, debts, and all economic contracts are nominated in money. These monetary contracts both guarantee and maintain the liquidity of money over time. Second, wages are contracted in monetary terms, also helping to maintain money's full liquidity. These wage contracts are rigid over some time, contributing to keeping the prices in aggregate, and thus the purchasing power of money, stable. Third, economic authorities always try to keep steady the cost of living, and they do so in monetary terms, which is also important for conserving money's liquidity and purchasing power.

The two elasticities of money make it a special asset in the economy. The three complementary factors of the third peculiar attribute guarantee and reinforce the liquidity and purchasing power of money over time. Together, these three attributes not only preserve money's liquidity premium, l, above money's carrying cost, c; they also secure a stable, or at least only a sluggishly decreasing, return on money in the form of pure liquidity, l, over time. This peculiar return is exclusive to money; thereby, all other variable-income assets have their return limited by money. If the return on these assets does not compensate for the risk of handing money in, they will not be purchased. The condition of capital goods is even worse, because their return, which is always uncertain, must reward not only the liquidity of money itself but also the return paid by interest rates charged on financial assets, which are less liquids than money but are more easily and cheaply converted into cash than any capital asset.

This is Keynes' general theory of money. It fills the last empty space in *The General Theory's* puzzle. He developed his monetary theory in a very original manner. More than simply fitting it into his monetary economy of production, Keynes offered to economics a deep and novel understanding of the nature of money itself. He explained why money is a convention, why this convention matters in keeping a given currency as money over time, and why this convention is neither taken for granted, tax-driven nor constant. The continuity of this convention depends on how monetary authorities manage money's elasticity of production in relation to the demand for it. Keynes also explained why money is never neutral, unlike how neoclassical economics understood it. It is because of the special properties of money that "a monetary economy, we shall find, is essentially one in which changing views about the future are capable of influencing the quantity of employment and not merely its direction" (Keynes, 2013d, p. xvi).

This chapter and the last six have explored *The General Theory*. Aware that it might have not been easy to follow each piece of the puzzle and the connections between them, Keynes restated the logic of the book in Chapter 18 of *The General Theory*. Following his lead, in the next chapter, we do the same, briefly recapitulating the picture that Keynes painted in his *magnus opus*. Hopefully, this restatement will help you to confirm your understanding of the pieces of *The General Theory* and the logic linking them and see why Keynes' book is irreplaceable in the economic theory.

Reference

Keynes, J. M. (2013d). *The General Theory of Employment, Interest and Money: The Collected Writings of John Maynard Keynes*, vol. VII. London: Royal Economic Society and Cambridge University Press.

11
ECONOMIC DYNAMICS EXPLAINED

A Summary of *The General Theory*

By now, all the important components of *The General Theory* have been revealed. We unpacked them to make their meaning and logical connections apparent. In Chapter 18 of *The General Theory*, Keynes reiterated the logic of the book, synthesizing the debate that had gone before. From Chapters 3 to 17, excluding a few chapters where he discussed specific points of neoclassical economics (like Chapter 14) or the procedural methods used in the book (such as the choice of the relevant units and the meaning he gave to concepts not free of ambiguous definitions in economics, as found in Chapters 4–7), Keynes explained piece by piece the relevant variables of his theory. Having presented each particular determinant of the economic system, in Chapter 18, near the end of the book, Keynes induced his *general* theory from the *particular* dots of *The General Theory*.

We especially emphasize *general* and *particular* because Keynes only generalized his theory after he had explained all the relevant pieces of it. In Chapter 2, we talked about induction – the method of acquiring knowledge by inducing a general conclusion from particular instances – as Keynes' method. Hence, it seems that Keynes not only used induction as his investigative method in *The General Theory* but that he also drove readers through the book by making them reason inductively. Remember that Keynes was interested in induction not because he saw any superiority in it as a scientific method, but because he saw it as the fundamental mechanism of human thought.

Keynes earned his bachelor's degree in mathematics at Cambridge in 1905. Three decades later, in *The General Theory*, he used simple mathematical parlance, stripped of formal language, to systematize the general conclusions of his theory. This is why he referred to types of variables in the book, which he calls the given, independent and dependent variables. The independent variables are the explicative ones; they set the economic system in motion and their movements mainly determine economic activity. Givens are variables that influence the independent

DOI: 10.4324/9781003287094-15

variables, but not to the point of determining them. In fact, these givens are not constant. However, their changes are incapable of producing big shifts in the economy in the short term, so Keynes did not take them into account. The dependent variables are those explained by the independent variables. Explaining them was Keynes' intention in *The General Theory*. The movements of the dependent variables are outcomes of the dynamics of the economy as set by the independent variables.

The dependent variables of *The General Theory* are the volume of employment, which corresponds with a certain volume of production and national income. The independent variables that explain the volume of employment are the propensity to consume, the marginal efficiency of capital, and the interest rate. These three determinants contain psychological components, namely, propensity (to consume), expectations (of prospective yields in the marginal efficiency of capital), and preference (for different degrees of liquidity). Two other factors have a close relationship with these independent variables but do not determine them. The first is the monetary salary, as negotiated between employers and employees. Salaries are key in determining prices (because wages are a paramount production cost) and the volume of money in circulation (because monetary wages are paid in money). The second is the action of central banks to manage the volume of money supply.

The General Theory has many given variables, namely, the skill and quantity of labor; quality and quantity of capital; existing state of technique; degree of competition; tastes and habits of consumers; disutility of different intensities of labor; supervision and organization activities; and the social structures determining the distribution of national income.

Taking these into account, movements in the independent variables cause alterations in the level of production and thus impact the dependent variables, employment and national income. These dependent variables are what Keynes intended to explain in *The General Theory*. Keynes was very much aware that in so complex a phenomenon as economics, generalizations accurate in all respects were impossible. Hence, he assumed that the independent variables – propensity to consume, the marginal efficiency of capital, and the rate of interest – could not be entirely exhaustive of all the particular variables conditioning the economy, still they were "the factors whose changes *mainly* determine our *quaesitum*" (Keynes, 2013d, p. 247, marks in the original).

The Logic of *The General Theory*: A Summary

The quaesitum of *The General Theory*, which are the theory's dependent variables, consists of employment and income. They are both outcomes of decisions to kick off production, from which Keynes in his book delivered a theory of production. Production is a result of investment, the key variable of Keynes' demand-led economics. Investment creates production and so it generates (1) employment, (2) income for workers, suppliers, and anyone who receives its outgoings (entrepreneurial expenditure is the income of those receiving it), and (3) a potential for greater social wealth. This greater social wealth coming from investment exists in potential, not necessarily reality, because it depends on whether entrepreneurs will succeed in having effective demand for their production. If effective demand does not match their supply, their losses mean that they personally will impoverish, that society is not becoming as wealthy as it could, and that full employment is an even more distant dream.

In Keynes' demand-led economics, the determinants of effective demand ultimately define production and, consequently, employment and income. The propensity to consume is one of the independent variables in *The General Theory*. Investment creates income and the latter explains consumption. The propensity to consume, in turn, sets the amount out of income that an individual turns into consumption. However, there is a fundamental psychological law that Keynes induced from the facts of experience: when an investment occurs and increases income, the variation of income is greater than the rise in consumption, and consequently, production grows more than consumption. Therefore, savings arise as a residue of greater income pushed by more investments. But savings are not consumption and entrepreneurs only invested because they wanted their production consumed. Thus, the paradox is that whenever entrepreneurs invest, they create not only greater national income but also greater aggregate savings.

What would balance the difference between the aggregate demand entrepreneurs expected when they invested but they did not accomplish because their very investments ensured greater savings? Once again, investment is charged with the task. Investment becomes responsible not only for igniting economic activity but also for keeping its dynamics stable over time. Consequently, the determinants of investment have a strong role in determining economic activity. Investment is determined by the marginal efficiency of capital and the interest rate, both of which are independent variables in *The General Theory*. They are, in fact, two rates of return. The first is the expected rate of return on capital goods, which is the yield entrepreneurs hope to gain if they invest in capital goods in the real economy. The interest rate is another rate of return, paid on debts negotiated in the financial system.

The marginal efficiency of capital is partly formed by things that can be known more or less for certain and partly by uncertain expectations of prospective yields upon which entrepreneurs can only hold a degree of confidence. The extent of entrepreneurs' confidence in their expectations depends on their subjective state of confidence in their conclusions about the future. Entrepreneurs' animal spirits are what excites them to confront the uncertain and unknowable forces of time and invest in illiquid capital assets. If they invest, they believe in the choices that guided their pursuit of greater future wealth. Production comes from this delicate balancing of factors determining investment decisions. Accordingly, the employment level and national income are social gains emerging from an entrepreneur's individual investment act.

This decision only happens if the uncertain calculus of the marginal efficiency of capital results in a hoped-for rate of return on capital goods at least equivalent to the rate of return paid on debts negotiated in the financial system. Hence, a rate of interest that is around the value of the marginal efficiency of capital is enough to disturb the purchase of capital goods, thus perturbing the rhythm and direction of economic activity.

The interest rate, in turn, results from how individuals are more or less willing to stay closer or farther from money (i.e., their liquidity preference). Money is the well of liquidity in the economy, to the point that the demand for liquidity *is* the procurement of money. The individual preferences for liquidity define whether individuals will supply money to the financial markets, an outcome of their speculative motive for demanding money, or prefer pure liquidity and hold money for precautionary motives. Interest rates outcome from the different liquidity preferences of individuals, resulting from their diversity of expectations about the gains they can have with financial assets.

The interest rate on money is the most important interest rate in the economy because money is a special asset, due to its negligible elasticities of production and substitution. Therefore, the supply of money is managed (thereby its negligible elasticity of production) and the demand for it is continuous (given its equally negligible elasticity of substitution). The managed supply of money implies that its return, which is its full liquidity, is steady; or, if it decreases, that it does so very slowly. Money thus possesses a continuing value that makes its price, the interest rate, an explicative variable of the rhythm at which employment and income expand. In this sense, the action of central banks toward money management and the level of monetary salaries are key elements in the management of the volume of money in circulation.

In short, the logic of *The General Theory* is as follows. The variables whose behavior Keynes explained were employment, production, and income. To clarify their determination, he developed a monetary theory of production in *The General Theory*. The expected aggregate demand creates production and generates employment and income. Thus, the level of employment (and of supply and national income) are demand-led. Consumption and investment are the two components of demand that define society's effective demand: the demand that actually happens in the economy. The effective demand, on one hand, depends on the propensity to consume. This propensity defines the aggregate level of consumption out of the national income. On the other hand, demand is also set by the marginal efficiency of capital and the interest rate as they define investment. The marginal efficiency of capital is the rate of return on capital goods. It is a ratio between the expected prospective yields of a capital asset during its lifespan and the investment cost. Hence, expectations of yields define the marginal efficiency of capital. The interest rate, in turn, is established in the financial markets in accordance with the different liquidity preferences of bear and bull agents who believe in a falling or rising market, respectively. The interest rate on money is the one that matters the most in the economy because money is a special asset. Its supply is managed by central banks in order to ensure that people will always demand it as unit of account, means of exchange, and reservoir of value. While everyone accepts money, it remains the full liquid asset in the economy. As such, if individuals facing uncertainty demand money in order to retain the safety conferred by liquidity instead of spending it to purchase capital goods, money affects the creation of jobs and income. Therefore, money is never neutral to economic activity; it can change both its cadence and direction. This is the logic of *The General Theory*.

The Sub-Normal Economy

You might be wondering have psychological factors, like propensity, expectations, and preference, too important a role in Keynes' economics? You are right to ask. Keynes saw economics as a moral science. As such, it always deals with human behavior, which is what builds this thing that we call an economy. Eliminate humans from the earth and there would be neither an economic system nor economics. No economic system is natural; all are human-made. To Keynes, economics was moral in the sense that the economy is built from the humanity of the women and men who construct it as they try to organize their social interactions and provide for their material needs. The natural traits of individuals in *The General Theory* are actual and irrevocable psychological aspects of human beings, but they do not make the economy nor economics something natural.

In neoclassical economics and in other theories it inspired, the economic system would have an optimal equilibrium point around which the economy always is. Their theoretical frameworks are devoid of the observable psychological aspects of individuals. Moreover, they suppose the existence of so-called natural economic variables, such as a natural product, natural interest rate, natural unemployment, or natural monopoly. Curiously, in these theories, markets are perfect and their invisible hands self-regulate the economy, with full employment, to the best possible economic equilibrium.

In Keynes' economics, these psychological aspects are central and according to them, the economy is liable to abrupt changes of course. However, we do not see violent fluctuations hourly. Crises happen, of course, as was vividly demonstrated in 1929, 1932, the 1970s, at the end of the 1990s, 2001, and 2008–2009. However, crises do not occur every day, nor have they led to the substitution of monetary economies of production with any other system in the last decades. Two are the reasons for this: State economic action and the economy's own forces.

As presented in the first chapters of this book, Keynes first started advocating economic management by economic authorities to help stabilize the economy in his 1923 *A Tract on Monetary Reform*. Thereafter, his calls for State economic action never stopped, nor his own practical work in shaping the world economy, especially after World War I onward. Keynes built his schematic synthesis of *The General Theory* using given, dependent and independent variables to map the variables that economic authorities could influence or administer. However, as economic policing was not the subject of *The General Theory*, Keynes talked too little about it in the book, aside from comments on monetary policy.

Nevertheless, he argued about some elements intrinsic to the economy and irrespective of governments that prevent it from often being devastated by strong slumps. He listed four of these elements. First, the multiplier is usually greater than unity, but not by much. Thus, increasing investment does not cause employment and income to grow out of control. Second, variations in either prospective yields or interest rate do not violently change the marginal efficiency of capital. Strong inflections in the marginal efficiency of capital are the cause of the crisis, as Keynes explained in Chapter 22 of *The General Theory*. They originate in sharp and rapid reversion of expectations that spread among individuals and cause a convention to form that expects a bad economic future. These movements are the well-known bandwagon effect, which is closely associated with economic crises. Although they occasionally happen, the common path of the economy can handle shifts in both prospective yields and interest rate not causing acute variations in the marginal efficiency of capital. Third, changes in the employment level do not cause a big variance in salaries. Costs and prices are thus stable, helping to build stability in the economy. Fourth, the system has a series of forces that act in different directions over the course of the economic cycle. For instance, consumption decreases less than income in recessions, and so a deep decline in aggregate consumption is avoided. The lifespan of capital goods acts in the same direction. As some capital assets grow old, investments to recuperate them or to buy new ones add effective demand to the economy. Governments also tend to increase their expenditures in times of recession rather than in booms, because widespread unemployment asks for their action to alleviate people's hardship. As governments expend, their spendings provide people with income and allow them to continue as consumers. This effective demand reduces the depth of the crisis.

The economy occasionally undergoes booms and depressions, the extreme borders of the economic territory. But average human behavior usually makes the economy stay at a midpoint far from these extremes. Social institutions, such as contracts, laws, and governments, also set limits on individuals' behavior, and consequently on the whole society, which facilitate stability around this midpoint. Therefore, Keynes' standpoint at the end of Chapter 18 of *The General Theory* deemed the normal economic stance to be sub-normal, bearing involuntary unemployment and staying quite beneath its growth potential, though not suffering from recession either. This sub-normal economic activity, Keynes argued, "seems capable of remaining in a chronic condition of sub-normal activity for a considerable period without any marked tendency either towards recovery or towards complete collapse" (2013d, p. 249).

Although this sub-normal situation is the common stable path of the economy, there is not much to celebrate. Keynes named it sub-normal instead of normal because a sub-normal situation wastes productive resources that could otherwise be employed to generate income. Take Brazil as an example. As this book is written, in mid-2022, the rate of unemployment in the country has been above 10% of the economically active population for six and half years, since January 2016. From 2016 to 2021, Brazil's average GDP growth was 0.25% (and even if you remove the pandemic year of 2020, the number is still not outstanding: 1.1% GDP growth per year). Brazil has been expanding its production less than it could normally be doing. Laborers are willing to work and look for job, but the country has not been creating them sufficiently. This is the sub-normal condition to which Keynes was referring.

References

Keynes, J. M. (2013a). *A Tract on Monetary Reform: The Collected Writings of John Maynard Keynes*, vol. IV. London: Cambridge University Press.

Keynes, J. M. (2013d). *The General Theory of Employment, Interest and Money: The Collected Writings of John Maynard Keynes*, vol. VII. London: Royal Economic Society and Cambridge University Press.

12

FINAL ELEMENTS OF *THE GENERAL THEORY*

Keynes devoted the final chapters of *The General Theory* to discussing elements that he deemed subsidiary to the development of his economics. Four of these elements, which we will discuss in the following sections, are the effects of variations in wages, employment function, a theory of prices, and trade cycles. We will also look at the social philosophy that Keynes advanced in *The General Theory*. These topics feature in Chapters 18–22 and 24 of that book. We do not study Chapter 23: it is a collection of theoretical issues that Keynes debated to show their differences with his theory. Although interesting, the chapter does not add any new theoretical element that justifies our scrutiny of it here.

It is worth mentioning that, in this chapter, the ideas and explanations are not presented as linearly as in the previous chapters. Keynes explained the central aspects of *The General Theory* in its first 18 chapters. After that, he explored a variety of specific points, such as wages, prices, and trade cycles, because they were – and still are – hot topics in economics. He then went on to present a social philosophy in the final remarks of *The General Theory*. In his economics, markets were not self-regulated, and the State should not possess the means of production, so he advanced a social philosophy that stated that governments and private initiatives should cooperate to cope with the disturbances that strike the economy occasionally. Keynes presented these topics without connecting them except to the economics he developed in the first 18 chapters of *The General Theory*. We will follow his lead below.

Changes in Money-Wages

Some chapters ago, we talked about the two postulates of classical economics to explain that neoclassical economists believed, first, that flexible wages guarantee automatic adjustments of the market, and, second, that workers cause

DOI: 10.4324/9781003287094-16

unemployment by not accepting reductions in their nominal wages. If workers did not agree with lower monetary wages, and unions existed to enforce this position of theirs, they were voluntarily consenting to stay idle, thus making persistent unemployment in the economy voluntary.

The neoclassical idea underlying the notion that the market adjustment process emerges from a lower nominal wage is as follows. A lower wage reduces the marginal cost of production and, thus, prices. Since prices and aggregate demand have an inverse relationship, lower prices increase demand, and the latter, in turn, enhances output and employment. When employment increases, wages follow suit and production as a whole becomes costlier, thereby raising prices. However, the total level of employment is greater than before. In conclusion, if workers accept lower monetary wages, the economy ends up better overall, with more employment than before.

Keynes did not accept the neoclassical view. In his theory, employment is not a self-fulfilling desire that depends only on whether workers accept lower wages that stimulate entrepreneurs to hire them. Keynes created the concept of involuntary unemployment, which is the usual economic case. Laborers look for job vacancies at the existing nominal wages, but nobody hires them. Keynes explained that real wages did not determine unemployment – in fact, real wages are hard to calculate; how many times have *you* assessed your precise real income, as neoclassical economics say you do? After showing the insufficiency of neoclassical theory, Keynes explained that effective demand explains employment.

In Chapter 19 of *The General Theory*, Keynes analyzed the neoclassical maxim that lower wages imply greater employment. Based on his economics, the causal chain from lower wages to higher employment runs through effective demand. To proceed with his analysis, Keynes asked two questions. The first was: keeping stable the determinants of effective demand, would lower wages cause less unemployment? Keynes answered that they would not. Even if the determinants of effective demand are constant, the community's capacity to demand reduces as wages fall. If entrepreneurs employ workers to increase their production, effective demand will fall short of supply. If lower wages were to increase employment, expectations of greater consumption and investment would be needed; but no one would rationally expect so, because effective demand cannot increase when aggregate income reduces as wages become lower.

The second question that Keynes asked was: how would lower wages affect, first, the components of effective demand and then employment? Unlike the first question, now the determinants of effective demand are no longer constant. Keynes gave seven answers, which are, briefly:

(1) If nominal wages decrease and prices follow suit but the income of other factors that enter the production cost remains stable, transferences of income happen. With prices going down, businesspeople's proceeds reduce. However, their financial liabilities are charted with fixed interest rates, thus entrepreneurs' debt burden rises. In this sense, there is a transference of income from

businesspeople to rentiers. But rentiers are wealthy people whose propensity to consume is low. The transference of income to them does not increase aggregate consumption, effective demand, investment, or employment. In that instance, lower wages do not increase employment then.

(2) If the economy is open to external transactions, lower wages ensuring lower prices would make the country's products cheaper for the rest of the world. Exports then increase. This stimulates investment and the creation of jobs. Thus, hereby lower wages can increase employment.

(3) Although lower nominal wages cause better trade balance, as in item (2), the trade terms (the ratio between the export and import prices of a country) worsen. The trade balance improves because cheaper prices cause the country to sell a greater quantity abroad. But cheaper prices also reduce the price of each thing that the country sells abroad against the price of products that it buys from foreign traders; thereby trade terms deteriorate. In that case, the reduction of wages might not improve employment.

(4) If money wages go down today but are expected to increase soon, entre- preneurs invest and employ. Lower costs today, and expectations of greater income when wages increase before long, encourage entrepreneurs to invest. However, the opposite will happen if businesspeople expect further reductions in wages following the initial decrease. The analysis is thus ambiguous, mean- ing that investment following lower salaries can either increase or decrease.

(5) In a scenario in which central banks keep the money supply stable, lower monetary wages, prices, and income would reduce the transaction motive for demanding money. Therefore, a certain amount of spare money would be used for speculative purposes, increasing liquidity in the financial mar- ket and lowering the interest rates. Accordingly, investment and employment would increase. Nevertheless, if wages and prices are expected to rise, short- and especially long-term interest rates would swell and restrict investment and, consequently, employment. Again, this analysis reaches an ambiguous conclusion.

(6) Nominal wages are not, in fact, the minimum wage or any other wage whose value is unique and standardized in the economy. Money wages vary between industries and economic sectors. Falling wages in one industry do not push down the wage of other industries. One specific industry might see greater employment following a wage reduction, but it is hard to generalize this out- come to the whole economy. Hence, the reduction of wages does not neces- sarily or generally improve employment.

(7) Price reductions caused by the contraction of wages increase the financial ser- vices of indebted entrepreneurs, as explained in item (1). This factor disincen- tivizes investments on its own, but the situation can get worse. Entrepreneurs can become insolvent and bankrupt depending on their financial burden in relation to the reduction of their proceeds that comes from lower prices. The bankruptcy of businesses would inevitably be accompanied by more unem- ployment. Moreover, governments can also see their debt burden increase if

prices decrease. If they want to stabilize their debt by rising taxes, businesses, and accordingly employment, might be affected.

In the end, most of the answers favorable to the argument that lower wages could generate investment and employment are, in fact, ambiguous in their possible outcomes. Only item (2) is unambiguous; in items (4) and (5) while lower wages can increase investment, the prevailing economic condition may also curb it. Conclusions unfavorable to the belief that lower salaries ensue bigger investments dominate Keynes' reasoning, as illustrated by the answer to the first question as well as replies (1), (3), (6), and (7) to the second question. The bottom line of Keynes' argument is that no one should expect lower wages to cause greater employment; it can happen, but the greater likelihood is that it will not.

To conclude Chapter 19, Keynes questioned neoclassical economics' defense of flexible salaries as the means of economic adjustment. Unsurprisingly, Keynes believed that short-term rigid monetary salaries are important to price stability. This, in turn, is key to building people's confidence in a country's currency. In this sense, stable salaries help monetary policy in its task of keeping prices steady and convincing people that the country's money is trustworthy.

Keynes also discussed the close connection between a flexible monetary policy and a flexible wage policy in terms of their impacts on money supply. Monetary, nominal wages are paid in money. Therefore, salaries and the volume of money in circulation move in concert. In that case, Keynes asked, what would be better: an economic policy of flexible wages or flexible monetary policy? As we know, Keynes formulated the best explanation of money that economics has ever had; and, of course, he advocated for a flexible monetary policy. Four reasons explain his choice.

In the first place, there is no means to assure an even reduction in wages in all industries and sectors. An uneven wage reduction inflicts social costs, wastes, and injustices and so is undesirable. Second, a fair and even reduction of income does not apply solely to nominal wages, but to all types of income. It is impossible to guarantee an equitable decrease in all incomes; equally, it is impossible to balance between the different social classes the consequences of lowering nominal income, and this is undesirable too. Third, lower salaries and prices while the central bank maintains the volume of money imply greater spare money as the need for it for transactions diminishes. More money will flow into the financial market, and the interest rate will reduce. This is good for investment. However, as explained in items (1) and (7) previously, lower prices in the face of stable financial commitments increase the debt burden of businesspeople and put their investments on hold. Fourth, the answers to Keynes' two questions earlier indicate that the relationship between lower wages and employment is uncertain. As explained earlier, it would be a mistake to expect that decreasing wages cause more employment.

If a flexible wage policy may barely deliver what the neoclassical economists promised, Keynes defended a flexible monetary policy on the grounds that it represents a better policy. In the sense discussed here, which focuses on the improvement of employment, a flexible monetary policy signifies central banks lowering the base rate of the economy by swelling money supply. An interest rate drop will stimulate consumption and, especially, investment, resulting in a boosted effective demand that nurtures employment. Moreover, particularly for the debt burden of business-people, a lower interest rate will soften their debt load (and can also stimulate more sales and improve their proceeds). More investment and job creation are thus the probable result. All in all, Keynes concluded that a flexible monetary policy is better than a policy grounded on flexible wages. A policy led by the latter is worse not only because it is unlikely to deliver employment but also owing to the reasonable probability that prices will become unstable if such a policy takes effect.

It might sound strange today to think of a flexible wage policy. But the neoclassical economists, both in Keynes' time and ours, favor fully flexible wages. This explains why the world has seen so many liberal labor reforms since the 1970s, along with the demobilization of workers' unions. Despite this, nominal salaries are still rigid. In practice, flexible wages are unworkable; how could entrepreneurs and workers change and chart wage contracts every day? The cost of this is unbearable, as are its economic consequences, from business planning to price stability and monetary policy. Keynes was aware of the practical problems that would emerge if a policy of flexible wages were tried; he also understood that wages were not actually flexible. Neoclassical economics idealized economics by arguing for impossible things like flexible wages; Keynes strongly refuted this and advanced a theory that saw reality as it was – and as it remains.

The Employment Function

In Chapter 20 of *The General Theory*, Keynes wrote the employment function, which is a simple mathematical equation that sums up the determinacy of effective demand on employment. As we well know by now, effective demand determines employment. Let us remember that N means employment and D demand and these two variables are positively related; they move alike. The employment function is as follows:

$$N = f(D).$$

Keynes warned in Chapter 20 that it should not be taken as true that every time effective demand increases, it necessarily increases employment. He assumed this simplification to facilitate the exposition of *The General Theory*. However, in Chapter 20, he relaxed this assumption. Of course, effective demand still determinates employment and the relationship between them is unavoidably positive, but it might not be linear: in certain circumstances, effective demand increases *without* correspondingly increasing employment. There are four reasons for this.

(1) When individuals' incomes grow, their greater consumption is not proportionally distributed among the goods and services they habitually consume. Some goods and services are more wanted or needed, and they are consumed

at a greater rate than other products. Hence, effective demand does not grow evenly between industries.

(2) The second motive is related to the first. If greater effective demand is made on an industry whose supply can expand without needing to employ more workers, employment will not rise. We have talked about elasticity before. It is the response of one variable to a disturbance caused by another variable, like the determinacy of effective demand over employment. In this sense, the elasticity of production demonstrates how production answers to effective demand. This response varies between industries. Some industries only can expand production by hiring workers; these are labor-intensive industries, often related to the supply of services. Other industries are more technology-based, or capital-intensive, and can enlarge production without necessarily engaging more laborers. The response of employment to effective demand depends on the elasticity of production in the industries that receive the greater effective demand. The more the new effective demand goes to labor-intensive industries, the better the result for employment.

(3) If industries anticipate a new wave of effective demand toward them, the better the result for employment. Anticipation means that businesses have more capacity to plan and reply to the greater procurement of their products.

(4) The fourth reason is related to stocks. The greater they are, the worse it is for employment. Companies with big stocks neither gear up for greater production nor employ more workers.

In general, expansions of effective demand will split into greater production and prices. The elasticities of both production and price are tested as effective demand moves. One rare and particular case among the innumerable possible positions of these elasticities is that of inelasticity of production. This is a rare case of full employment. The theoretical framework of neoclassical economics was built upon full employment wherefrom Keynes argued that neoclassical theory was not a theory of production or employment, but of distribution on conditions of full employment. Moreover, at full employment, any greater effective demand (e.g., one resulting from government expenditures) will cause inflation in the neoclassical model. But full employment is an exceedingly rare case – and it is the only one in which neoclassical theory can explain the economy. The usual economic case, Keynes taught, sees the presence of unemployed resources and both price and quantity (production) moving to respond to effective demand. The extent to which price and production shift depends on the current economic circumstances. Once again, Keynes' theory places the economy in the position of being subject to several equilibria, whereas neoclassical theory is entirely predicated on the (seldom historically encountered) state of full employment.

The Theory of Prices

In neoclassical economics, the theory of value exists as part of the real economy, where production and distribution happen. The value of things results from the marginal production cost plus the stage of the elasticity of supply. The latter is, in fact, an inelasticity of production as neoclassical economics assumes that the economy is always at full employment. However, prices are not a phenomenon of the real economy, but rather of the financial sphere, as the supply of money, a financial event, determines them. Hence, price and value are disconnected in neoclassical economics; money defines prices, whereas the conditions of production set the value of products. In conditions of equilibrium in an undisturbed economy, the price of products is their value. But if for any reason a shock, such as government deficits arising or central banks increasing the supply of money, affects the equilibrium, the growth of money supply ensures higher prices but without causing any change in the value of products.

Keynes disagreed with such a watertight division of the economic system. The real and financial economic sectors are intertwined. Values as well as prices are decided on the real economic side, and a greater supply of money can change both or neither, depending on the circumstances. Moreover, Keynes pointed out that the correct analysis is not of the strict relationship between money and prices; the correct causal chain must include effective demand. For example, take the case when governments – which are the source of all evil in neoclassical economics – increase money supply. The correct examination of the impacts of this act must first consider the response of effective demand to the growth of money in circulation; then the analysis needs to account for how well the supply structure of the economy, which includes elasticity and cost, suits the greater effective demand. After that, it is possible to check the responses of prices and production.

As stated earlier, the normal case is that both quantity and price move as more money in circulation swells effective demand. This, in turn, creates more employment. All pieces move together, the speed of each relying on how the growth of effective demand matches the capacity of production. The causal chain from more money in circulation to greater effective demand, employment, wages, production, and prices is subject to five interdependent considerations. These considerations are (1) that effective demand does not change proportionally to money supply; (2) the productive factors are not homogeneous, meaning that when employment increases, workers of different skills are employed, implying changes in costs and fickle returns of scale; (3) productive factors are specialized and not interchangeable. The production of one product might become inelastic while workers (and other productive resources) are still unemployed, but they do not suit the production of this product whose supply became bottlenecked; (4) wages and prices start increasing before full employment; and (5) the production factors' costs change disproportionately.

Keynes did not accept any sort of binarism in analyzing the responses of price and production to shifts in effective demand. Therefore, the well-known neoclassical credo 'if the government issues money it generates inflation' is a lie to both Keynes and economy reality. It can happen, but it will not occur always. Moreover, those who adopt the Keynesian perspective but say that Keynes did not address the supply side of the economy are mistaken. Keynes stated that the economic system is demand-led, but you must not see in this any negation of the importance of the supply side.

Lastly, as Keynes only talked about prices lately and subsidiarily in *The General Theory*, you could think that he belittled inflation. This is not the case, although Keynes was indeed more concerned with delivering a theory of production in which money had a key role to play. Still, in Chapter 21 (and incidentally in Chapter 20) of *The General theory*, Keynes discussed inflation.

On the one hand, Keynes explained that upward adjustments of wages are discontinuous owing to the psychology of workers and the bargains struck between them and employers. Hence, wages increase as employment grows, but according to a different ratio. In view of that, Keynes called the price variations that accompany any discontinuous increase in wages semi-inflation. He named this process semi-inflation because he was reticent to name every price rise inflation. Keynes was absolutely against high inflation; in both *A Tract* and *A Treatise*, the other two Keynes' books discussed in the second part of this book, he dealt with inflation. He believed that healthy economies would see prices rising modestly; no concern and fussy were necessary if prices went up a little, say 2–3% in advanced economies and 4–5% in developing countries, under the strict vigilance of central banks.

On the other hand, Keynes' definition of full employment is as follows:

> we have full employment when output has risen to a level at which the marginal return from a representative unit of the factors of production has fallen to the figure at which a quantity of the factors sufficient to produce this output is available.
>
> *(2013d, p. 303)*

At full employment, a swelling effective demand cannot raise production because of aggregate inelasticity of production; thus, the greater effective demand only and proportionally increases costs and prices. Keynes called this rare, though possible, situation true inflation. The semi-inflationary upswing of prices occurs hourly and is accompanied by increasing employment and wages, but workers involuntarily unemployed remain. At full employment true inflation holds; to Keynes, this is the particular case wherein neoclassical theory explains the economy.

The Trade Cycles

In Chapter 22 of *The General Theory*, Keynes presented his trade cycle theory, better known today as the economic cycle. Cycle, in economics, means precisely what it signifies in any other aspect of life: it is a movement that first goes in one direction, then loses force, and finally reverts its direction. Within the economic cycle, there is one essential element, well-known to the public: the crisis. Crisis is the fast, unpredictable, and violent substitution of an ascension phase of the cycle for a recessive phase. Every time you hear conversations about the economic crisis, the talk is about this strong inflection in the phases of the cycle.

In the cycle, all explicative elements of effective demand are relevant. However, the marginal efficiency of capital is preponderant; its oscillations enforce the cycle's phases. The other determinants of effective demand bolster the cycle, but they do not create it; the marginal efficiency of capital accomplishes this job. The oscillations of the marginal efficiency of capital are cyclical, Keynes argued. During an economic boom, entrepreneurs' expectations are too high and encourage them to invest. They underestimate the abundance of capital that comes with their overoptimism. The cost of investment increases as quickly as investment takes place. Credit becomes abundant during the boom, "during a boom the popular estimation of the magnitude of both these risks, both borrower's risk and lender's risk, is apt to become unusually and imprudently low" (Keynes, 2013d, p. 145). The intense demand for funds in the capital market lifts the interest rate. Yet entrepreneurs expect such good prospective yields that the marginal efficiency of capital does not decline.

However, at some point, despite the hard pace of investment, sales grow slower than entrepreneurs expected, yields are less than anticipated, and stocks begin to rise unexpectedly; in like manner, the once high expectations are superseded by disillusion with an economy that is overinvested because individuals were previously overoptimistic. Expectations collapse and overthrow the marginal efficiency of capital. The fall of markets is abrupt and violent, as is the installation of the crisis. Banks' state of confidence breakdown and credit becomes restricted. The flee to liquidity spreads throughout the economy; the interest rate increases in accordance with the greater liquidity preference of individuals, aggravating the crisis as it adds more depressive effects to investment. On top of that, fallen markets cause, through the negative wealth effect, the impoverishment of financial investors, thus decreasing society's marginal propensity to consume, especially in countries where the wealth effect is an important source of funds for consumption.

In the crisis, central banks must reduce the base interest rate of the economy. Although necessary, low interest rates are insufficient to start the recovery – remember that there is nothing automatic in Keynes' theory, so low interest rates do not directly equate to greater investment. The economic recuperation will depend on the restoration of entrepreneurs' confidence, an element well outside economic authorities' control. Time helps to overcome the crisis. The lifespan of capital goods requires investment to recover the equipment. In the slump, stocks involuntarily multiply, but after a while, they reduce until more production is needed to regularize aggregate supply. Nevertheless, the way out of the crisis necessarily passes through the improvement of expectations and, consequently, of the marginal efficiency of capital.

At the end of Chapter 22, Keynes wondered if the interest rate should rise to avoid overinvestment. He concluded that it should not. Although a high interest rate is more efficient at moderating a boom than alleviating a slump, the prevention of crises should not involve elevating interest rates. The analogy for a high interest rate is that it is like a medicine that cures patients by killing them. The true cure is to be found in improving the marginal propensity to consume, even with an income distribution policy, so that consumption will sustain effective demand if investment vacillates. The very term overinvestment, Keynes reasoned, was somewhat inappropriate. There can be no overinvestment if economies have involuntary unemployment and social capital below their potential, thus still offering opportunities for profitable investments. In this sense, overinvestment would be, at best, a bad name used to describe a characteristic of the ascendant phase of the cycle.

Before concluding, a curiosity. Keynes is remembered as the economist who talked about the imminence of cycles and crises in capitalism. However, this is not because of his theory of cycles, but because of the determinacy of uncertainty and expectations on investment. Nevertheless, Keynes dedicated a chapter of *The General Theory* to develop a theory of cycles, and in other passages before Chapter 22, he briefly discussed the credit cycle as well. For example, in Chapter 12, he said, "For whilst the weakening of credit is sufficient to bring about a collapse, its strengthening, though a necessary condition of recovery, is not a sufficient condition" (2013d, p. 145). Notwithstanding Keynes had his own theory of cycles, it is not his cycle theory that is most recalled in the Post Keynesian tradition, but that of Hyman Minsky. A well-known follower of Keynes, Minsky developed his financial fragility hypothesis in the 1970s, which then became his famous financial fragility theory in the 1980s. The final form of his theory can be seen in Minsky's 1986 *Stabilizing an Unstable Economy*.

Minsky went further than Keynes in the microeconomic analysis of financial positions assumed by both banks and real sector companies. His theory also thoroughly explained how these microeconomic financial positions can cause macroeconomic impacts, either boosting economic growth in booms or pushing the economy to its collapse in slumps. He created the term financial fragility to express the idea that a good financial position, which he named hedge, can cyclically and quickly become a bad one, which he suggestively named Ponzi. Minsky was a pioneer in theorizing how financial markets were growing crisis-makers because of financial leverage and innovations. In memory of his contributions to comprehending the financial determinacy over economic cycles, the term Minsky Moment was created and used to describe the 2008 subprime financial crisis, in both academic and non-academic media.

The Social Philosophy Toward Which the *General Theory* Might Lead

At the end of Chapter 22, Keynes made clear that it is best for the economy to stay in a semi-boom or semi-slump, that is, in between the phases of the cycle without incurring strong oscillations. In Chapter 24, Keynes offered guidelines on how to attain this. By means of what he called the socialization of investment, he requested that the State cooperate, in all possible ways, with private initiative. By socialization, Keynes did not mean, as he clarified, a broad governmental ownership of capital goods; he was not talking about socialization of the production means. His socialization involved governments attempting to reduce the risks that private agents face when they invest. Individual investment builds social wealth. When an investment goes well, society wins. If it fails, society does not gain, yet nobody loses as much as the entrepreneur. Keynes argued that socialization of investment was a way to collectivize the risks of businesses, just as their individual success constructs social prosperity. This socialization is mostly done by economic policies. Incidentally, Ferrari-Filho and Conceição (2005) offered an original and creative interpretation of socialization of investment. In their view, this socialization also means the creation of an institutional, political, and social environment that favors private investments. If States create this good environment for business, they will reduce uncertainty and assure less investment risks.

At the beginning of this book, we said that Keynes did not theorize economics for the sake of idle contemplation. He wanted to understand economics in order to act in the economy to improve people's lives. The socialization of investment is proof of this. Keynes argued for a rational level of State cooperation with private initiative. He believed neither in self-regulating markets organizing society nor in the State setting aggregate supply. The truth, he trusted, lay between these two poles, in a system where the private initiative is free to make the economic choices it wishes accompanied by governments backing these choices.

Keynes ended *The General Theory* with a social philosophy because he was trying to change the philosophical ground of economics from a neoclassical, individualistic selfish, and utilitarian basis to one that was still individualistic but at least founded on more altruistic and collectivistic ideals. Keynes was trying to save capitalism from its two greatest evils, namely, involuntary unemployment and the unequal and arbitrary distribution of wealth and income. He was trying so in an era when totalitarian governments were nearby him, in the USSR, Germany, and Italy.

Although Keynes did not see individualistic capitalism as a perfect system, his desire to reform it was due to his belief that this system was good for maintaining individual liberty of choice as well as rewarding private actions that, in turn, built fruitful social outcomes. Individual behavior was capitalism's foundation. Therefore, Keynes believed that although this system was inherently individualistic, it did not need to be completely selfish. Individuals could still act to seek personal pleasure and reward while remembering that their acts formed the economic whole while that whole conditioned their acts. For instance, it is impossible for entrepreneurs to succeed alone; they *need* other people to consume their products to achieve their individual goals.

Nevertheless, to coordinate initiatives that individuals uncoordinatedly undertake in the economy, Keynes argued for State economic action – an argument for which he remains famous. Although throughout *The General Theory*, he hints every now and then at some economic policy prescriptions, it is not in this book that his framework for economic policing is to be found. His views on monetary policy are more evidenced in that book, but not his positions on fiscal, income, and exchange rate policies. Not even in Chapter 24, where he argued more extensively in favor of government action, will the reader find clues of what he had in mind for economic policing. Instead, those views lie in several other works of him.

The next part of this book will summarize Keynes' economic policy prescriptions. It also presents his views on the structure of the State and discusses his notion of economic development. The next chapters therefore present the means by which the State can cooperate with the private initiative as well as the ideal point at which *The General Theory* might arrive: economic development.

References

Ferrari-Filho, F. and Conceição, O. A. C. (2005). 'The Concept of Uncertainty in Post Keynesian and in Institutional Economics', *Journal of Economic Issues*, 39(3), pp. 579–594. DOI: 10.1080/00213624.2005.11506835.

Keynes, J. M. (2013a). *A Tract on Monetary Reform: The Collected Writings of John Maynard Keynes*, vol. IV. London: Cambridge University Press.

Keynes, J. M. (2013b). *A Treatise on Money I, the Pure Theory of Money: The Collected Writings of John Maynard Keynes*, vol. V. London: Cambridge University Press.

Keynes, J. M. (2013c). *A Treatise on Money II, the Applied Theory of Money: The Collected Writings of John Maynard Keynes*, vol. VI. London: Cambridge University Press.

Keynes, J. M. (2013d). *The General Theory of Employment, Interest and Money: The Collected Writings of John Maynard Keynes*, vol. VII. London: Royal Economic Society and Cambridge University Press.

Minsky, H. (1986). *Stabilizing an Unstable Economy: A Twentieth Century Fund Report*. New Haven: Yale University Press.

PART IV

Beyond *The General Theory of Employment, Interest and Money*

Economic Policies, State, and Development

If we randomly ask people in the street if they have heard, seen, or read anything about John Maynard Keynes, it is very likely that the replies be that he was an economist who talked a lot about crisis and State economic intervention. In addition, the respondents might also say that Keynes was "that economist who defended public deficits and said that it is ok to live with some inflation."

Let me tell you how I first "met" Keynes. Back in 2001, I was in the last year of high school, in Araxá, Brazil, the city where I was born in 1984. One day, in history class, I was taught that Keynes was the intellectual mentor of Franklin Delano Roosevelt's New Deal and his theory was based on using public deficits to stimulate the economy. When I started studying economics at the Federal University of Uberlândia, in Uberlândia town, also in Brazil, I was lucky enough to have professors who introduced me to *The General Theory*. When I first read this book in 2004, it really surprised me to realize that Keynes barely talked about fiscal policy or the New Deal in it. For example, the term fiscal policy appears only eight times in the whole book; five of those eight times occur in four paragraphs over four pages in Chapter 8, when Keynes discussed tax policy. The word deficit shows up only twice in the book, while public debt appears four times, none of them in the book itself but in its second appendix, originally published as an article in *The Economic Journal* in September 1936, after *The General Theory* has been first published in February. Keynes occasionally mentioned government borrowings and the debt of some countries, but only in passing; the topic of public debt is not even a secondary matter in the book. Finally, Keynes mentioned the New Deal four times in *The General Theory*. Hence, my first contact with Keynes was not with him, but with a commonly held belief that remains prevalent, as though it somehow represented him.

DOI: 10.4324/9781003287094-17

In this part, we will present Keynes' economic policy prescriptions. The ideas revealed in the next chapters are entirely based on his own writings. Our intention here is to acquaint you with Keynes himself and show the common belief about him to be a nonsense. The next chapter, Chapter 13, accounts for fiscal policy; Chapter 14 presents monetary policy; and Chapter 15 explores the exchange rate policy. The economic policy framework that Keynes outlined is the main means wherewith he expected the State to act in the economy; many of his claims for an investment socialization consist of States undertaking his suggested economic policies.

Keynes requested State action throughout his main economic works, but he went further and advanced a description of his ideal State, which we will discuss in Chapter 16. Finally, Chapter 17 presents Keynes' notion of economic development. Development is the arrival point of Keynes' economics, toward which he wanted his theory to lead society. Keynes hoped that at the development stage, the economic problems of society would no longer be the main economic problem confronting mankind.

Finally, let us make one further thing clear. In some countries, the word government is commonly used instead of State, whereas others take the opposite approach. In this book, we will use State, but please understand it as being synonymous with government. Furthermore, by State, we do not mean a provincial governmental entity like those of subnational divisions of a country. Keynes created *macro*economics and suggested *macro*economic policies; thus, by State, we mean the national entity that manages the *macro*economic policy of the nation.

References

Keynes, J. M. (1936). 'Fluctuations in Net Investment in the United States', *Economic Journal*, 46(183), pp. 540–547.

Keynes, J. M. (2013d). *The General Theory of Employment, Interest and Money: The Collected Writings of John Maynard Keynes*, vol. VII. London: Royal Economic Society and Cambridge University Press.

13
FISCAL POLICY

Economic policies must pursue full employment and better income distribution, which are the two greatest evils of capitalism in Keynes' view. Economic policies should reach their aims by working in coordination: an economic policy alone is incapable of achieving full employment and improving income distribution. Within Keynes' economic policies prescription, fiscal policy is the most important of all.

Fiscal policy is composed of two policies: tax and public expenditure policies. The latter is direct effective demand, making it a powerful economic tool. The occasional mention Keynes made of public expenditure in *The General Theory* emphasized that governments are effectively demanding when they spend. In comparison, the interest rate, which is monetary policy's main tool, has only an indirect economic impact. Changes in the interest rate are central banks' attempt to influence agents' economic movements and the speed at which they move in the economy. As monetary authorities cannot control agents' behavior in an economy based on free initiative (like capitalism), they can only try to influence them. But the outcomes of central banks' actions are broadly uncertain. In contrast, when States invest, which is a fiscal action, they impact the economy directly. Let us see how Keynes outlined his fiscal policy framework.

Tax Policy

The function of fiscal policy's tax policy is, of course, to gather the resources necessary to finance State expenditures. Setting aside this obvious purpose of tax policy, Keynes' main preoccupations regarding taxation focused on three aspects. First, in Chapter 8 of *The General Theory*, Keynes considered the effects that changes in taxation could cause on consumption and effective demand given their repercussions for the propensity to consume. Keynes also pointed out the negative effects that a tax policy oriented to form sinking funds for public debt repayment could

DOI: 10.4324/9781003287094-18

cause. This is part of what today we call fiscal austerity. The more that States establish taxes to gather resources for sinking funds, the worse it is for effective demand.

Keynes' second concern with tax policy centered on the relationship between taxes and the distribution of income and wealth. We already know that Keynes considered unequal distribution to be one of the two greatest problems of capitalism (the other being the involuntary unemployment). Nevertheless, he believed that society should only compensate those who contribute to it, not those capable of adding something to the community but who have yet to do so. Society must reward its contributors and protect those who are incapable of producing or in need, such as involuntarily unemployed people. Hence, Keynes was not an egalitarian regardless of individuals' possible contribution to society. He was convinced that tax policy was a proper way to arrange social justice and better distribution, which would also enlarge effective demand.

Accordingly, tax policy is a tenet of the social philosophy that Keynes espoused in Chapter 24 of his *General Theory*. It explains why he protested so vehemently against rentiers and heirs and their unearned incomes (they are unearned because what rentiers and heirs earn from society is not equal to what they add to it). A special taxation levied on rentiers, Keynes argued, should target not only their gains but also some of their speculative practices in the financial market. In his words, "the introduction of a substantial government transfer tax on all transactions might prove the most serviceable reform available, with a view to mitigating the predominance of speculation over enterprise in the United States" (Keynes, 2013d, p. 160).

Third, Keynes required that the tax policy should not disincentivize investment. Taxation can affect investment in two ways. First, taxes and surtaxes are costs that lower the yields expected by entrepreneurs. Second, taxation can impact business confidence; this is the case, for example, with a fiscal policy managed to reduce public debt by repaying it with resources gathered by greater taxes. However, Keynes did not view taxes charged on businesses as necessarily negative. If they aimed to finance governmental policies that increase the propensity to consume, investment would respond positively. Keynes argued that the ideal administration of the tax policy should not inhibit the disposition of entrepreneurs to invest, but this should not be confused with exempting businesses from taxation. His claims were for a rational tax policy, focusing on weighing more on rentiers and heirs' unearned income, distributing wealth to fortify society's propensity to consume, and not creating disincentives to investment.

Public Expenditure Policy

Keynes' proposal for State expenditure policy is founded on a public budget segregated into two big accounts, namely, the ordinary or current budget and the capital budget. The task of the former budget is to fund the outgoings with which the State affords the public services it offers to the population it takes care of. Disbursements of money for the health system and for social security, education, public security, and others are enrolled in the ordinary/current budget. Keynes wanted this budget to be in equilibrium. If possible, surpluses should be encouraged, because they could pay for the expenditure of the capital budget, which is the essential element of Keynes' fiscal policy.

The capital budget enrolls State investment. It is the budget that stabilizes the economy. Keynes stated that the capital budget should have a long-term investment plan and its execution should be countercyclical to economic cycles. If the private initiative is investing, the disbursements of the capital budget can diminish to avoid inflation. If the opposite scenario is in motion, the capital budget acts inversely. If there should be a refutation of entrepreneurs' expectations and a collapse in the marginal efficiency of capital, the State should increase and accelerate public works. This is the idea driving a fiscal policy that automatically stabilizes cycles: it is a fast State action that tries to counteract the direction in which private initiative goes.

As discussed before, Keynes believed that keeping the economy in a state of continuous semi-boom or semi-slump was the best economic trend; he suggested that the worst economic movement is the roller coaster of successive growth and recession. It does not matter if the economy grows 10% in one year but stagnates by 1% in the following year and decreases by 1% two years hence. This is as bad a movement to entrepreneurs' outlook on the future as, say, three consecutive years of a mild recession. A GDP that oscillates too much hinders business people's planning ability. It is not only recessions that can blur expectations but also constant GDP oscillations. Therefore, Keynes preferred a state of moderate growth, whether of semi-boom or semi-slump, because the less the economy booms or slumps, and the more it stays between both, the better. Accordingly, Keynes proposed his countercyclical capital budget as a tool by which States could try to mediate countries' GDP growth as he trusted that "a long-term programme of a stable character should be capable of reducing the potential range of fluctuation to much narrower limits than formerly" (1980a, p. 322).

The funds to cover the capital budget's expenses come from the typical sources of public resources, namely, taxes. Although the capital budget has public funds specially and regularly allocated to it, surpluses of the ordinary budget should eventually step up the endowments of the former budget, especially if it undergoes deficits. Keynes was thus seeking to increase the funds available to enhance public investment as this would augment aggregate investment. Moreover, although profit is not the intention per se of the capital budget, it may occasionally occur. In this case, the "capital expenditure would, at least partially, if not wholly, pay for itself" (Keynes, 1980a, pp. 319–320). This would furnish more resources to the State, strengthening the overall fiscal policy stance.

Keynes' choosing of a capital budget that prioritizes investment rather than consumption is due to his belief that countries have not reached their potential capital stock. There remains investment to be made that could improve society's wealth and its aptitude to produce goods and services able to improve individuals' material life conditions. Once society has reached its wealth potential and the economy enters a steady-state condition, public policies directed to stimulate consumption will substitute the operation of the capital budget.

Some operational features for investment arising from the capital budget are listed below:

(1)   Public investment should never compete with private initiative. The purpose of the capital budget is to cooperate with private initiative, meaning that private and public agents can better cope with crises together than alone.

(2)   The capital budget must account for technical social investment. Kregel (1985) explains that this investment is especially important to the economy but too risky, long term, and expensive for private initiative to make it. This is typical of investment in infrastructure, such as ports, roads, and energy plants. Private initiative requires this infrastructural equipment as it is the base on which the productive investment of the economy is built. Nevertheless, the characteristics of this sort of investment are not attractive enough to make the private sector that needs it to invest in it. For the sake of the best economic activity, public investment must solve this paradox.

(3)   The capital budget must not focus on one business. Its investment plans should not create privileges and should be as horizontal as possible among the economic sectors. The own idea of investment being of a technical social nature protects the capital budget from being used for the purposes of a specific business. Associations of public and private capitals can occur, but always with the intention of producing social welfare.

(4)   Keynes proposed using the capital budget for automatic economic stabilization; automatic stabilization is not a tool of last resort. It aims to counterbalance the cyclical private forces that drive the trade cycles in the economy. If the capital budget does not avoid an economic slumping, it will obviously work as a rescuer of the private sector. But this means that the capital budget scheme has already failed in its effort to keep the economy stable. The function of the capital budget is to counteract, as contemporaneously as possible, the direction of private initiative attempting to maintain it between the boom and slump economic borders. In rather metaphorical words, the capital budget is like ships' ballast: it serves to balance things whose movements would become disastrously extreme if there was nothing to stabilize the swing.

The capital budget is an attempt to mediate the private forces that drive economic activity. The modulation of private forces has nothing to do with curtailing them. Keynes was not keen on self-regulating free markets, nor was he fond of central planification; in his view, neither worked. The former leaves no room for collectivity, which is inadequately seen as the mere sum of individuals. The latter leaves no room for private economic freedom; rulers, commonly dictators who praise themselves as the voice (and sometimes the mind) of collectivity, define all economic decisions. Keynes, who was a democrat, did not accept autocrats. In his view, States and the democratically elected people that govern them represent collectivity. Economic planification is nothing but a paroxysmal criticism of free markets, and both are equally radical in that they exclude something, either the

State or private initiative. Keynes favored the midpoint, in which the two big pro-
tagonists that form the economy, the State and private initiative, work together;
both collectivity and individuals should cooperate as none of them can be certain
of what the future will be.

The following metaphor summarizes Keynes' view. In the big, uncertain, and
uncontrollable economic ocean, where depending on the circumstances the main-
land can be either solid ground or a treacherous swamp, States are the lights that
help private ships to navigate; economic policies are the anchors that prevent them
from floating away; and the capital budget is the ballast that provides them with
stability. The job of the economic policy can fail. But, to Keynes, it is better to fail
trying to do something than to see the economy fail and do nothing justified by
the mistaken dogma that "the crisis makes market adjustments; the best businesses
survive." The problem with this blind view is that in economic crises much more
than just businesses die.

Public Deficit

As seen previously, Keynes' public budget proposal requested that the ordinary
budget be in equilibrium or surplus. Eventual surpluses would gather more
resources for the capital budget, to either finance more investment or balance this
budget if it were in deficit. Moreover, as time passes and some investments made by
the capital budget start to show profits, more resources will flow into this budget.
All in all, Keynes was arguing for an intertemporal balanced budget.

However, the widely held belief regarding Keynes' position on fiscal policy is
that he is the economist who had intellectually sponsored fiscal imbalances to boost
economic activity. But this is not him. The fiscal framework he suggested is the
one described earlier, in which the overall budget is mostly in equilibrium. He did
not say that a public deficit was required to operate a countercyclical fiscal policy.
In fact, Keynes saw public deficits as an expedient of last resort, used if the capital
budget failed to stabilize the economy. Keynes' position on fiscal policy in general,
and especially on public deficit and debt, is controversial even among his followers;
his critics also take these points to make criticisms of him.

The best strategy to remove the controversy is to check what Keynes himself has
said about these divisive topics. In his view, public deficits occur if "the volume of
planned investment fails to produce equilibrium" (Keynes, 1980a, p. 352); in this
case, "the lack of balance would be met by unbalancing one way or the other the
current budget. Admittedly this would be a last resort, only to come into play if the
machinery of capital budgeting had broken down" (1980a, p. 352). If doubts about
his view on public deficit remain, observe how clear he made it: "so very decid-
edly I should cut down all this and not lead the critics to think that the Chancellor
is confusing the fundamental idea of the capital budget with the particular, rather
desperate expedient of deficit financing" (Keynes, 1980a, pp. 353–354).

As for the public debt, Keynes explained that he would prefer it to result from
the capital budget. A public debt resulting from expenditure in the form of public

investment would produce future resources with which the State could repay, at least in part, its liabilities. Keynes intended, in this sense, that the State would "thus gradually replacing dead-weight debt by productive or semi-productive debt" (Keynes, 1980a, p. 277). Dead-weight debt is a sort of debt that does not produce the wherewithal for its future redemption.

Keynes had this position toward public debt and deficit based on the trio of uncertainty, expectation, and confidence. Keynes was well aware that public debt is the paramount financial asset in the economy, and so it is widely accepted as means through which States make monetary and fiscal policies. In addition, it is usually the asset that benchmarks all other financial assets in the economy. However, Keynes was also conscious of the fact that States and their governments cannot control the public opinion on public finance. Nor can they expect from people a deep knowledge of economics so that they could clearly know the differences between the public debt and their own private debt. Keynes illustrated this with his usual irony,

> Thus we are so sensible, have schooled ourselves to so close a semblance of prudent financiers, taking careful thought before we add to the "financial" burdens of posterity by building them houses to live in, that we have no such easy escape from the sufferings of unemployment. We have to accept them as an inevitable result of applying to the conduct of the State the maxims which are best calculated to "enrich" an individual by enabling him to pile up claims to enjoyment which he does not intend to exercise at any definite date.
>
> *(2013d, p. 131, marks in the original)*

People do not take the fiscal policy stance for granted. Their changing expectations and confidence concerning public deficit and debt can cause problems for the operation of economic policies. For instance, if a convention is in force that causes people to see the country's public deficit as too high, individuals will ask for greater interest rates to buy public bonds. The same can happen if the conventional belief becomes that the public debt has assumed too great a proportion of the country's GDP. Individuals can simply reject buying public bonds or, if they purchase them, do so by soliciting high interest rates. Both ways imply more expensive State borrowings and a more complicated economic policy operation. Furthermore, aggregate investment is also affected by the greater interest rates that are now charged on public bonds and, consequently, throughout the economy. Again, in Keynes' own words,

> This means, unfortunately, not only that slumps and depressions are exaggerated in degree, but that economic prosperity is excessively dependent on a political and social atmosphere which is congenial to the average business man. If the fear of a Labour Government or a New Deal depresses enterprise, this need not be the result either of a reasonable calculation or of a plot with

political intent; – it is the mere consequence of upsetting the delicate balance of spontaneous optimism. In estimating the prospects of investment, we must have regard, therefore, to the nerves and hysteria and even the digestions and reactions to the weather of those upon whose spontaneous activity it largely depends.

(2013d, p. 162)

The fiscal policy has a great discretionary maneuver capacity to deal with economic cycles, which is enhanced if governments are capable of grounding individuals' expectations. Keynes' public budget proposal functions in this direction. It is a kind of long-term contract between the State and society. Over time, people get used to how it works, and the more used they get, the smaller their suspicions about what the fiscal policy might become. For pushing private investment, this stable and confident relationship between private initiative and the State is indispensable. The big margins of discretion and maneuver held by the fiscal policy and the outstanding position of the public debt among all other financial assets in the economy provide the State with big economic power. But this power should not be confused with the State being the almighty actor in the economic system. Opponents of this idea can always argue that States that issue their own sovereign currency face no fiscal risk whatsoever, to which Keynes would reply "just as a moderate increase in the quantity of money may exert an inadequate influence over the long-term rate of interest, whilst an immoderate increase may offset its other advantages by its disturbing effect on confidence" (2013d, p. 267).

Keynes' non-hard-line worldview determined his posture in fiscal matters. He chiefly intended that the capital budget should prevent crises, but he knew that one way or another crises would occasionally happen. If expectations were so degraded as to make the capital budget fail, public finance would run deficits and States would see their debt increasing. In fact, public deficit and rising public debt were not exceptions in Keynes' day, but regular events in the economy, as they are still today. However, just because an event is recurrent does not exempt it from the effects of people's changing expectations and confidence. In light of that, in 1942, years after the publication of *The General Theory*, Keynes proposed his capital budget scheme and made clear how the State should operate it.

Minsky, whom we talked about in the last chapter, held a position on fiscal policy remarkably similar to Keynes. In Minsky's words,

there is nothing special about government debt, and a flight to quality can occur. For a foreign-held debt such a flight will lead to a deterioration of the currency on the exchanges; for a domestic debt the flight can lead to inflation and a need to pay ever higher interest rates to have the debt held.

(1986, p. 302)

Minsky also argued that governments could run deficits on some occasions, mostly during recessions; however, these deficits need to be temporary. More importantly than that, society must also *understand* them as temporary, enduring, at most, for as long as the event causing them lasts, "any deviation from a government budget that is balanced or in surplus must be understood as transitory – the war will be over, the resource development program will be finished, or income will be at the full-employment level" (1986, p. 303).

Keynes' mild opinion on fiscal policy contrasts with the perspectives of both neoclassical economics and Abba Lerner's (1943) functional finance, nowadays fostered by the upholders of Modern Money Theory (better known by its acronym, MMT). The former's standard position sees public deficit as the cause of all economic problems. In turn, savings, including public ones ensured by government primary surpluses, are the bases of economic progress. To refute this view, Keynes asked "Were the seven wonders of the world built by thrift? I deem it doubtful" (2013c, p. 134).

Abba Lerner's perspective goes in the opposite direction. It assumes that public deficits are no problem at all, at least until full employment is attained. As David Colander (1984) related, Keynes disagreed with Lerner. Colander (1984) quoted other people, such as Abba Lerner himself and Evsey Domar, to report Keynes' remarks. Quoting Lerner, Colander narrated "[Lerner saying] When I pointed out that the government could always induce enough spending by incurring deficit to income increases, he at first objected that this would only cause 'even more saving' and then denounced as 'humbug' my suggestion" (1984, p. 1572, marks in the original). Recounting Domar's version of the history, Colander added, "not only did Keynes call Lerner's statement 'humbug,' he also paraphrased Lincoln's 'you cannot fool all of the people all of the time'" (1984, p. 1573, marks in the original). Colander also described Keynes retracting his denunciation later, but afterward, he insisted that Lerner's theory was ideal and therefore impracticable. Taking again from Colander (a passage that is also published in Keynes (1980a))

> I recently read an interesting article by Lerner (1943) on deficit budgeting, in which he shows that, in fact, this does not mean an infinite increase in the national debt, since in the course of time the interest on the previous debt takes the place of the new debt which would otherwise be required. (He, of course, is thinking of a chronic deficiency of purchasing power rather than an intermittent one). His argument is impeccable. *But heaven help anyone who tries to put it across (to) the plain man at this stage of the evolution of our ideas.*
>
> *(1984, p. 1574, marks inserted)*

In conclusion, Keynes' fiscal policy proposal can be deemed pragmatic. He emphasized the importance of State expenditure, the outstanding position of the public debt among the financial assets in the economy, and that public deficits would regularly occur without causing major problems. Nevertheless, he positioned himself away from those who see public deficits as either the economic solution or the problem. In Keynes' proposition, public investments assume a distinctive character in the making of the public budget. Notably, they were responsible for automatically stabilizing economic cycles and keeping the economy in a permanent state of quasi-slump and quasi-boom. However, the budget proposals Keynes advanced were not put into practice. He developed them in 1942, amid World War II and on the eve of the Bretton Woods Conferences in 1944, in which Keynes was the chief proponent of reorganizing the international monetary and financial system; moreover, all this happened right before his death in 1946. Hence, he did not have much time to defend his fiscal policy viewpoints. Still, his own record of his proposals allowed us to recall them and state his fiscal policy framework.

A Brief Debate on Compulsory Savings-Based Income Policy

During World War II, Keynes held important positions, virtually working as a non-official Chancellor of the British Treasury, as Carter (2020) described. The war set two immense challenges. First, how could the United Kingdom finance the War? Second, how could society's consumption of non-essential goods be reduced in order to secure the production of the war materiel, which would equal a sizeable proportion of that country's GDP? Witty as Keynes was, he perceived a third problem: how could the full employment of wartime be maintained after the war? Keynes presented these problems and the solutions he forged to them in his *How to Pay for the War* (Keynes, 2013e).

The regular solutions to these problems were threefold. Taxes were the first option. But they are chiefly levied on the working class as it is the most populous social class in the country. This would be unfair, Keynes argued, because workers were manufacturing the war materials. Government borrowings were the second alternative. However, Keynes' argument was that this was risky: it depended on individuals' marginal propensity to consume, on the one side; on the other, it also relied on their liquidity preference, which would not be keen to buy public bonds of an over-indebted country like the United Kingdom during the war (in the war's immediate aftermath, the British national debt equaled 250% of the country's GDP). The third choice was inflation. The government could issue money and demand the war materiel it needed, but Keynes warned that printing money would trigger greater governmental demand but supply was bottlenecked by war needs. The printing money strategy would only work with decreased aggregate consumption. If not, inflation would occur. Concordantly, injustice accrues as workers lose with rising prices whereas businesspeople gain, worsening income and wealth distribution.

The three problems were on the table, and Keynes pointed out the issues that would outcome if the three standard solutions were practiced. But he would never have missed the opportunity to offer a creative and original solution to this conundrum. He proposed compulsory savings to be charged on workers. These savings would gather resources to finance the State war effort; at the same time, they would reduce consumption and avoid the detour of the country's production capacity from the war requirements.

Keynes fought taxes and inflation as solutions to the problem because they were unjust to workers, but were not compulsory savings unjust too? Unlike taxes and inflation, savings were a fund of resources; thus, they were, in fact, a workers' stock of wealth. They were mandatorily used to buy an asset: British public bonds. This meant that the Treasury could finance the war and workers could form a stock of wealth. Moreover, Keynes oriented some accessory conditions to the plan to ensure that it would not be inauspicious to workers and, consequently, to distribution. For example, he suggested that lower-income people be exempt from saving. The collection of savings was progressive, with upper-income workers contributing more. Inflation should be controlled to inhibit the corrosion of the real value of the workers' stock of wealth.

After World War II, when the first signs that effective demand was cooling down appeared, the stock of wealth formed by compulsory savings levied on workers would return to them. Their greater income would increase their propensity to consume and help maintain effective demand stability. However, where would the resources to return savings to workers come from? Nothing has implied that the State would have had more resources than before the conflict. To solve this problem, Keynes proposed taxing businesses, mainly those that had extraordinarily gained during the war. The war yielded them windfall profits; therefore, income had been distributed in their favor. In the course of the war, the windfall gains provided businesses with funds to expand their productive capacity, something that a country in battle needed. After the war, though, it was time to redistribute income in favor of those who had labored to build the war materiel, the workers.

Compulsory savings were the means the State used to handle income and wealth distribution, first from workers to the State and next to businesses; after the war, in accordance with the economic cycle, the distribution went from businesses to the State and thence to workers. There remains a question: would greater taxes charged on businesses disincentivize investment as they depress the marginal efficiency of capital? Yes, this could happen, Keynes acknowledged. But he was betting in another direction. He was looking to the devolution of the compulsory savings to a huge mass of workers and the boost on the propensity to consume that it would cause. This, he believed, would animate investment.

The functional expression of Keynes' plan was that the State management of income and wealth distribution would usefully handle economic cycles. In the background of his proposals, Keynes was confident that the absence of cycles could aid in the construction of social peace in Europe. He knew that the period between the two World Wars lacked social peace and its aftermath was disastrous – and he alerted the world about the risk of this disaster in his *The Economic Consequences of the Peace* (Keynes, 2012). But by now, reader, you should be curious: was Keynes' plan implemented? Yes, it was, and it worked well. In Carter (2020), this history can be found in greater detail.

References

Carter, Z. D. (2020). *The Price of Peace: Money, Democracy and the Life of John Maynard Keynes*. New York: Random House.

Colander, D. (1984). 'Was Keynes a Keynesian or a Lernerian?', *Journal of Economic Literature*, 22(4), pp. 1572–1575.

Keynes, J. M. (1980a). *Activities 1940–1946: Shaping the Post-War World – Employment and Commodities. The Collected Writings of John Maynard Keynes*, vol. XXVII. London: Royal Economic Society and Macmillan.

Keynes, J. M. (2012). *The Economic Consequences of the Peace.* Summit: Start Publishing.

Keynes, J. M. (2013c). *A Treatise on Money II, the Applied Theory of Money: The Collected Writings of John Maynard Keynes*, vol. VI. London: Cambridge University Press.

Keynes, J. M. (2013d). *The General Theory of Employment, Interest and Money: The Collected Writings of John Maynard Keynes*, vol. VII. London: Royal Economic Society and Cambridge University Press.

Keynes, J. M. (2013e). *Essays in Persuasion: The Collected Writings of John Maynard Keynes*, vol. IX. London: Royal Economic Society and Cambridge University Press.

Kregel, J. (1985). 'Budget Deficits, Stabilisation Policy and Liquidity Preference: Keynes's Post-War Policy Proposals', in Vicarelli, F. (ed.) *Keynes's Relevance Today.* London: Macmillan, pp. 28–50.

Lerner, A. (1943). 'Functional Finance and the Federal Debt', *Social Research*, 10(1), pp. 38–51.

Minsky, H. (1986). *Stabilizing an Unstable Economy.* A Twentieth Century Fund Report. New Haven: Yale University Press.

14

MONETARY POLICY

Monetary policy is the State action that intervenes in the economy by means of money and finance. Central banks, such as the US Federal Reserve System, the UK Bank of England, and the Brazilian Central Bank, are the State entity responsible for handling monetary policy. Monetary management is a twofold task. On the one hand, it takes care of the national currency. On the other hand, it also uses money as a tool to accomplish effects on other economic variables, such as employment and growth.

Keynes dedicated a lot of his attention to monetary policy in *The General Theory*, more than he devoted to fiscal policy. He had a main concern in mind: the operation of monetary policy is delicate because it does not directly interfere with the economy. In fact, monetary policy processes its effects by means of how agents respond to variations in monetary conditions, especially in the interest rate. But agents may respond differently from expected by central banks, either in an opposite direction or not even changing their positions. In contrast, the capital budget-based fiscal policy is a direct intervention in the economy as State expenditures are effective demand straightforward. In this sense, although monetary policy is a powerful economic instrument, central banks might easily err while undertaking it, thus failing in achieving their objectives.

In comparison, in Keynes' time, the neoclassical economists suggested for monetary policy a very restrictive conduction. They believed that countries should attach their currency to a gold standard regime. Coupling the national currency with gold (or even with an external currency) automatically limits the operation of monetary policy. The range of possible central bank actions becomes constricted to maintaining the parity between the national currency and gold (or a foreign currency). Therefore, monetary management is left without any instrumental autonomy to deal with domestic matters. Even if the country does not ballast its currency to gold or foreign money, neoclassical economics suggested that central banks should never

DOI: 10.4324/9781003287094-19

use money as an economic tool. They should follow the quantity theory of money to set the volume of money in circulation. If they skip doing so, the economy will arrive at inflation only and yet without changing anything in the real economy. Money is neutral to economic activity, neoclassical economics assumed. The attempt to use it in the pursuit of increasing employment and GDP is worthless.

In this book, we accompanied Keynes' struggle, from 1923 to 1936, to quit thinking in neoclassical terms and deliver an economics in which money had a role to play. While departing from the neoclassical position on money, Keynes also abandoned its views on monetary management. As we saw in Chapter 3, although in his 1923 *A Tract on Monetary Reform*, Keynes was still believing in the correctness of the quantity money theory in the long term, he still asked for an active monetary policy to balance short-term fluctuations. On the road to *The General Theory*, Keynes fully rejected the quantity theory of money and requested an active monetary policy whose actions were no longer restricted to balancing short-term abnormalities. It is in this Keynes' full-fledged monetary policy that we delve now.

The Goals of Monetary Policy

The ultimate goals of monetary policy are to reach full employment and better income distribution. However, central banks and their monetary policy cannot fulfill this task alone. Full employment and better income distribution are such challenging things to achieve that only the coordination of all economic policies could help to direct the economy's prow toward them. Thus, there should inexorably exist coordination between the economic policies. In this sense, what monetary policy really pursues is five goals, which are under its immediate responsibility. It is by fulfilling these five immediate goals that central banks contribute to the other economic policies in attaining their ultimate objectives.

The first immediate goal of monetary policy is to maintain prices stable. Despite the held belief that Keynes did not concern with inflation, he did concern with it. He devoted *A Tract on Monetary Reform* and *A Treatise on Money* to understanding price dynamics, and he, although subsidiarily, also analyzed price in *The General Theory*. Low and controlled inflation is a normal thing in economies. But if inflation gets unbridled, it causes three negative effects on effective demand and threats job creation and GDP growth. These negative effects are (1) the deterioration of consumers' purchasing power, which reduces consumption; (2) distribution worsens and decreases consumption as inflation favors entrepreneurs' gains; and (3) inflation blurs the long run, disturbing entrepreneurs' outlooks on future and hampering their investment plans. Therefore, central banks must keep prices stable.

The second direct goal of monetary policy is to stabilize the economy's external sector. This goal is twofold. On one side, monetary policy must deal with the exchange rate. There is a specific policy to handle the exchange rate, the exchange rate policy, which we will see in the next chapter. But monetary policy also participates in the job of keeping the exchange rate stable, as instabilities in it have negative consequences. An oscillating exchange rate complicates entrepreneurs' ability to manage their businesses; for instance, if they focus on selling their production in external markets, their proceeds will change along with the exchange rate variations; however, changing proceeds is all entrepreneurs do not want for their enterprises. Moreover, if it gets more expensive to buy a foreign currency in the country, all imported inputs' prices rise, triggering inflation and deteriorating effective demand by reducing consumers' purchasing power. This is, too, bad for business. Thus, the exchange rate is an essential macroeconomic price in any country. Hence, Keynes asked for monetary policy to help the exchange rate policy preserve the exchange rate as stable as possible.

On the other side, when central banks manage their interest rate, they alter the relation between domestic and external interest rates. Differences between these rates change the destiny of international capital flowing around the globe. If the country's interest rate becomes bigger than the external rates, the country will attract foreign capital. But if the domestic rate gets lower than the average interest rate prevailing abroad, capital will move away from the country. Whether capital leaves or enters the country, it requires the conversion of domestic currency into foreign money, and vice versa. This conversion changes the volume of money circulating in the economy, so it can affect the country's term structure of interest rates. As the financial system and the real economy are not watertight, an unstable yield curve will destabilize the whole economy, especially because of its depressive effects on investment. Monetary policy must prevent this from happening.

The third immediate aim of monetary policy is to hold liquidity stable. Lacking or excessive liquidity causes interest rates to fluctuate. However, variations in the interest rate must occur not because central banks mistakenly managed liquidity, but because bull and bear agents had different opinions. Furthermore, an excessive liquidity might create financial leverage and an overwhelming financial bubble in the financial system. In turn, liquidity shortage runs in the opposite direction. It lifts interest rates and recessive pressures grow strong in the economy. Thus, the administration of liquidity is a crucial duty of central banks.

The fourth direct responsibility of monetary policy is to guard financial stability. History tells us about financial crises, like the well-known events of 1929, the 1990s, and 2008. As repeatedly affirmed, in Keynes' economics, money is not neutral and the real economy and financial system are not isolated from each other. Hence, the outcomes of financial crises are not circumscribed solely to the financial markets: they affect the real economy. Financial instabilities cause businesses to fail. They destroy jobs and lead the economy to recession. The duty of monetary policy to watch over financial stability has been growing in importance as the world is continuously getting more financialized and thus more prone to financial bubbles and crises.

The last task of monetary policy is to take care of expectations. Although Keynes did not use the term, central banks' conduction of expectations is today called forward guidance. In *A Treatise* and *The General Theory*, Keynes explained the importance of agents' expectations about the future trend of interest rates. If agents' outlooks on the future interest rate are disordered, central banks lose their power to influence the economy's yield curve. The central banks' interest rate is the most important interest in the economy. For no other reason than this paramount importance of central banks' interest rate, it is the economy's base interest rate, which benchmarks all other interest rates in the financial markets. The economy's yield curve departs from the base rate. Such an importance obligates central banks' monetary policy to manage their interest rate with very much care because individuals always have an eye staring at it. Stabilization of expectations means that monetary policy should not confuse society's opinions about the future direction of the base interest rate. In this sense, the central bank should inform what it has pondered to decide on each new base rate level.

Paradoxically, informing society about the future trend of the base interest rate does not mean that central banks must previously announce every future interest rate they will set at each meeting of their monetary policy committee. If monetary policy previously notifies what the interest rate will be, it will lose room to deal with changing circumstances. In view of that, agents' different opinions about the future interest rate provide monetary policy some margin of maneuver. If all agents unanimously agree with a certain base rate, monetary policy becomes dominated; if central banks do not establish this certain rate, agents' expectations can disarray and turn monetary policy unfruitful. The idea of central banks driving expectations signifies that they need to build a kind of expectation range that limits what agents should wait for the future of the interest rate. To sum up, expectations are so important to monetary policy that Keynes (2013d, p. 203) alerted,

> thus a monetary policy which strikes public opinion as being experimental in character or easily liable to change may fail in its objective of greatly reducing the long-term rate of interest. . . . The same policy, on the other hand, may prove easily successful if it appeals to public opinion as being reasonable and practicable and in the public interest, rooted in strong conviction, and promoted by an authority unlikely to be superseded.

You might have observed that in the five immediate goals of monetary policy, the word *stability* appeared. In an economy in which opinions matter so much but are so subject to change, the economic policy must not be another source of instability. This idea was already presented in the last chapter, where the topic was fiscal policy. Monetary policy has an even bigger responsibility in terms of not messing with agents' expectations. The direct consequences of central banks misleading agents' expectations are increasing interest rates that can depress investment. In addition, the task of monetary policy is more complicated if compared to fiscal policy because monetary management works based on how it influences agents' decisions. Thus, the central bank is always fine tuning its measures, checking what agents are thinking, and trying to guide their opinions. Monetary policy can never assume that it has agents on its radar for granted. It is the opposite: to a considerable extent, the work of central banks focuses on ever-maintaining agents within the radar of monetary policy.

The Instruments of Monetary Policy and Their Transmission Channels

Monetary policy has three main tools through which it tries to, first, influence agents' behavior, second, impact effective demand, and finally, affect the economy. These instruments are regulation, debt management, and the interest rate. Regulation is the set of laws that define what agents can and cannot do in the markets of the financial system. For example, the requirements of compulsory reserves from banks, a well-known monetary policy tool, are regulation; macroprudential measures and the Basel accords that regulate the banking system are regulation too.

Regulation transmits its effects to the economy both directly and indirectly. As far as it permits certain financial transactions and prohibits others, it directly restricts agents' behavior in the financial markets. The indirect effect of regulation is the assistance it gives to the management of the central bank's interest rate. Regulation reduces the need for the interest rate to modulate financial institutions' leverage given that the regulatory framework diminishes the range of risky financial transactions that can be made.

The other instrument of monetary policy is debt management. In their usual operation in the money market, central banks use short-term debt to control and stabilize their base interest rate, which forms the base for short-term interest rates in the economy. However, central banks try to influence the medium and long-term segments of the term structure of interest rates only by using their short-term interest rate. This mismatch of maturities can difficult the operation of monetary policy. Agents' medium- and long-term expectations can imply a high yield curve, sufficient to hinder investment. Moreover, in moment of stress, such as crises, the yield curve can become very volatile, which also encumbers investment. With debt management, monetary policy operates with short-, medium-, and long-term debt, in pursuit of directly influencing the term structure of interest rates in all its extension, especially the long-term segment, which immediately competes with the marginal efficiency of capital. Thus, debt management provides monetary policy with more power in its attempt to format a yield curve that stimulates investment.

The main function of debt management is the assistance it gives to the short-term interest rate that central banks manage in their monetary policy. As debt management takes place, the base rate of monetary policy no longer works alone in the endeavor of trying to manage the whole extension of the yield curve. Hence, debt management reinforces the transmission channels of the interest rate, which is the other tool of monetary policy. Moreover, debt management can also help in financial and liquidity stabilities. They enable central banks to make debt twists that furnish liquidity to specific segments of financial markets, deleverage and make less risky the balance of financial institutions, and avoid fast debt deflation.

Keynes proposed debt management in the 1936 *The General Theory*. In 1945, he proposed it again (Keynes, 1980a). Six decades later, after the 2008 crash, central banks of advanced economies started undertaking debt management. Although national treasuries usually adopted debt management, central banks also took it on as an innovation. Part of the famous quantitative easing that the US Fed operated counted on debt management. Also, Fed's so-called debt twist operation, which the Bank has occasionally operated since 2011 to lower long-term interest rates, is debt management. To confront the economic negative effects of the COVID-19 pandemic, central banks worldwide largely used debt management. Better late than never, Keynes would be happy to see that what he proposed in the 1930s and 1940s finally took place 60 years later.

The interest rate is the main monetary policy tool. Keynes deemed it "the governor of the whole system" (2013c, p. 189). Central banks' interest rate is the price at which they negotiate money (also called reserves) with the banking system; they set their interest rate aiming at achieving the immediate goals under their direct responsibility. Beyond base interest rate, central banks' interest is also named policy rate, because their interest rate is their outstanding monetary policy instrument.

What central banks really set in their monetary policy is the target of interest rate they believe will reach the goals they follow. To make the targeted interest rate effective, central banks have two operations at their disposal. First, the discount window, through which central banks furnish reserves to banks. On these loans, central banks charge the policy rate, thus actualizing it. Nowadays, the discount window has been losing importance for monetary policy operations. It is still in practice, but banks use the discount window to borrow money from central banks as a last resort, mostly when liquidity gets scarce during crises.

The second way by which central banks actualize their targeted base rate is open market operations. This is the main operation of monetary policy. It occurs by central banks buying and selling securities, especially short-term public bills, to control the quantity of money circulating in the money market and, consequently, in the other markets of the financial system and in the economy. As central banks control the quantity of money in the money market, they thus define the primary price of money, which is the base interest rate, at the level they want. The predominance of open market operations accrues from the fast, flexible, and fine-tuning money control that they offer.

Once open market operations effectively set central banks' base interest rate, five channels transmit the effects of this policy rate to the economy. The first is the expectation channel. We have broadly mentioned how expectations matter to the interest rate setting. When individuals make their economic decisions, they always try to guess which interest rate will prevail in the future. Therefore, a good and ordered state of expectations is required for the transmission of the interest rate's effects to the economy; otherwise, as monetary policy moves the policy rate, it will not drive agents' opinions and decisions in the direction it intends to lead the economy. Expectations are so crucial to monetary policy that they can be seen as a channel that enables and works before the operation of the other channels.

In Chapter 15 of *The General Theory*, Keynes richly and widely explained why expectations are essential to monetary policy. Keynes' own words illustrate such importance,

> In general, however, a change in circumstances or expectations will cause some realignment in individual holdings of money;–since, in fact, a change will influence the ideas of different individuals differently by reasons partly of differences in environment and the reasons for which money is held and partly of differences in knowledge and interpretation of the new situation. Thus the new equilibrium rate of interest will be associated with a redistribution of money-holdings. Nevertheless it is the change in the rate of interest which deserves our attention. The latter is incidental to individual differences, whereas the essential phenomenon is that which occurs in the simplest case. Moreover, even in the general case, the shift in the interest rate is usually the most prominent part of the reaction to a change in the news. The movement of bond prices is, as the newspapers are accustomed to say, "out of proportion to the activity of dealing";–which is as it should be, in view of individuals being much more similar than they are dissimilar in their reactions to news.
>
> *(2013d, pp. 198–199, marks in the original)*

If monetary policy is properly ordered and drives expectations adequately, the second channel through which the interest rate will transmit its effects is the portfolio channel. Changes in the interest rate cause agents to shift the assets they carry in their portfolios. As agents swap assets, buy new ones, and sell others, they alter liquidity and interest rates in different markets of the financial system. Therefore, the interest rate channels its effects to effective demand throughout the economy.

The third channel is the wealth effect. It accrues from changes in agents' wealth associated with shifts in the market prices of assets. As monetary policy shifts its base interest rate and agents change their portfolios, the current market-to-market price of assets alters, either increasing or decreasing and turning investors richer or poorer, respectively. These changes in assets' price will cause variations in effective demand to the extent that individuals are accustomed to realizing eventual gains to increase consumption. Monetary policy can try to reduce aggregate consumption by causing losses in the market-to-market prices of assets; oppositely, central banks can attempt to foster consumption by reducing its base rate to stimulate higher market asset prices. The greater the wealth effect in an economy, the more efficient the monetary policy.

The credit channel has six transmission mechanisms via both credit and capital markets of the financial system. In the credit market, the interest rate processes its effects on consumption in three ways. First, changes in the interest rate alter the disposition of individuals to consume using credit as they shift the cost of borrowing. Second, different interest rates imply different individuals' allocation of consumption over time. A low interest rate reduces the opportunity cost of current consumption as individuals will not be yielding high interest gains if they save and invest instead of consuming. A high interest rate works the other way around and turns present consumption expensive. Third, in terms of the relation between the credit market and businesses, the interest rate channels its effects on the cost of working capital loans to firms. For example, the higher the interest rate, the more expensive working capital credit lines, and the more restrictively businesses administer their cash flows.

Three are also the credit channels operating in the capital market. The first is the opportunity cost that the interest rate signifies to investment. Do you remember that the interest rate and the marginal efficiency of capital determine investment? Thus, at each interest rate level, there will be a viable level of investment. Nevertheless, the interest rate is, too, an effective cost to investment; this is the second mechanism that channels monetary policy from the capital market to the economy. Interest rates charged on funds that finance investment plans compose businesses' investment cost and enter the calculation of the marginal efficiency of capital. Hence, not only is the interest rate a subjective opportunity cost to the marginal efficiency of capital, but it is also an effective cost that changes the gains expected by entrepreneurs. Finally, if financial investors have insufficient resources to settle financial transactions, they can, say, borrow to lend. They borrow resources to buy financial assets which they bet will yield more than the cost of their borrowings. These transactions, which are usually made by investors who are more prone to risk, can become unviable if interest rates increase. High interest rates oblige the return offered by the assets for the purchase of which investors are borrowing money to be also reasonably high. However, when high interest rates dominate the economy, stagnation, or more likely recession, tends to occur.

The last mechanism through which monetary policy channels its effects is the exchange rate. By means of the difference between the domestic and the external interest rates that monetary policy can manipulate, central banks try to appreciate or depreciate the country's currency in relation to a relevant external currency. To fight inflation, central banks usually tend to increase their interest rate attempting to appreciate the domestic currency by making it stronger. However, if central banks seek to boost the economy, they will lower their base interest rate to depreciate the country's currency.

Monetary policy has many goals but only a few instruments to reach them. It is a powerful State economic tool; however, its operation is not an easy task. The main monetary policy tool, which is the interest rate, acts indirectly in the economy. It changes relative prices; thereby it tries to motivate agents in one or another direction. However, it is not because the task of monetary policy is hard that it should be guided by chance or under absolute restriction. Monetary policy must be flexible to deal with changing expectations of agents and fickle economic circumstances. But to achieve their intents, central banks must be transparent, clear in their communication, and committed to the achievement of the best economic conditions.

Keynes also requested that the staff members of central banks should be technical individuals, who understand the difficulties of their tasks. However, as Biböw (2002) showed, Keynes rejected an, in today's jargon, independent central bank, which could decide the targets it will seek independent of what society chooses as best for itself. As Keynes (1982) himself has shown, he advocated for what is today called the operational autonomy of central banks. In light of that, the democratically elected government sets the economic desires to be pursued by the State economic entities, like the central bank and the treasury. Thereafter, the technical members of the central bank should manage monetary policy to reach these desires based on the people's election of the government.

References

Biböw, J. (2002). 'Keynes on Central Banking and the Structure of Monetary Policy', *History of Political Economy*, 34(4), pp. 749–787.

Keynes, J. M. (1980a). *Activities 1940–1946: Shaping the Post-War World – Employment and Commodities: The Collected Writings of John Maynard Keynes*, vol. XXVII. London: Royal Economic Society and Cambridge University Press.

Keynes, J. M. (1982). *Activities 1931–1939 World Crises and Policies in America and Britain (The Monetary Policy of the Labour Party): The Collected Writings of John Maynard Keynes*, vol. XXI. London: Royal Economic Society and Cambridge University Press.

Keynes, J. M. (2013a). *A Tract on Monetary Reform: The Collected Writings of John Maynard Keynes*, vol. IV. London: Cambridge University Press.

Keynes, J. M. (2013b). *A Treatise on Money I, the Pure Theory of Money: The Collected Writings of John Maynard Keynes*, vol. V. London: Cambridge University Press.

Keynes, J. M. (2013c). *A Treatise on Money II, the Applied Theory of Money: The Collected Writings of John Maynard Keynes*, vol. VI. London: Royal Economic Society and Cambridge University Press.

Keynes, J. M. (2013d). *The General Theory of Employment, Interest and Money: The Collected Writings of John Maynard Keynes*, vol. VII. London: Royal Economic Society and Cambridge University Press.

15
THE EXCHANGE RATE POLICY

Another policy that States should undertake in Keynes' view is the exchange rate policy. It helps the economy to achieve full employment and better income distribution by dealing not only with both the exchange rate itself but also with the country's balance of payment (which is the accounting system that records all transactions between a country and its external partners), and the exchange rate market where the exchange rate is determined. The relative position of each domestic currency in the international monetary and financial system is very unequal. Just a few currencies are accepted internationally, the US Dollar, Euro, British Pound, Japanese Yen, and a couple of others. Among these currencies that circulate worldwide, none shares the importance of the US Dollar. Therefore, the monetary policy of the United States is the exchange rate policy of most countries in the world, as they have the US Dollar as their most important international foreign money. Every time the Fed administers its Fed Funds rate, it affects the global flows of the US Dollar and changes the exchange rate between the US Dollar and other domestic currencies.

The exchange rate is not just the simple price at which two domestic currencies are exchanged. In fact, it has major macroeconomic implications for the economy. A substantial portion of inputs that a country uses to manufacture its GDP comes from abroad and is thus affected by the exchange rate. A weak, depreciated domestic currency makes the country's production costlier and pressures inflation. Notwithstanding this inflationary problem, a country that has no reserves in foreign currency can be hit by a currency crisis; in the extreme case, it cannot even carry external transactions. These currency crises are usual in the history of emergent countries and even of some advanced economies.

Moreover, it does matter not only the price (the level) of the exchange rate but also its volatility (variation) as constant and intense fluctuations in the exchange rate disturb the economy. Exchange rate volatility hinders entrepreneurs' capacity

DOI: 10.4324/9781003287094-20

to predict their export prices when they pursue to sell their output in foreign markets. Exchange rate volatility also causes the cost of producing goods and services with imported inputs to fluctuate. Businesses can hedge their external cost. But within intense exchange rate fluctuation, the cost of this protection also increases and affects businesses. Further, exchange rate oscillations exacerbate the foreign exchange risk that international investors face when they move productive or financial capital around countries.

Thus, the exchange rate is too important a macroeconomic price to be guided by chance. In Keynes' days, the gold standard regime was proposed and implemented as a solution to the issues emerging from the exchange rate. In his early days as an economist, Keynes went along with the proposers of the gold standard. However, by the early 1920s, he began criticizing this foreign exchange arrangement because of its rigidity to deal with changing economic circumstances, the cost it implies to produce economic adjustments, and the lack of autonomy that it foists to monetary policy. Keynes recognized that this regime benefits price stability, but its problems did not compensate for this benefit. Monetary policy and its coordination with other economic policies can handle price variation using other less costly means.

The goals of Keynes' exchange rate policy proposal are twofold. First, this policy needs to pursue external equilibrium. Second, it is responsible for tackling exchange rate volatility. Nevertheless, the operation of the exchange rate policy must guarantee autonomy to monetary policy. Keynes' concern with the relationship between monetary and exchange rate policies was due to the possibility of central bank's constant usage of their base interest rate as a tool to manage the exchange rate. Situations can occur where monetary policy sets its base interest rate to get along with external issues, like attracting external capital to avoid currency crisis, reduce exchange rate volatility, or offset inflation. But if the central bank's interest rate becomes too attached to foreign questions, it can lose sight of local issues threatening the domestic economy.

If neither a floating regime in which the exchange rate buoys freely, nor the rigid gold standard, what did Keynes propose for the exchange rate policy? Once again, Keynes' economic policy prescriptions are at the midway; in this case, his proposal is the midpoint amid the rigidity of the gold standard and the full liberty of floating exchange rates. Keynes suggested an administered exchange rate, in which the exchange rate between the domestic currency and the most important foreign currency for the country's international transactions should remain stable.

But notice that an administered exchange rate is not a fixed exchange rate. In monetary economies of production, circumstances are liable to change as fast as agents' opinions, which drive their liquidity preference, vary. Therefore, the managed stability of the exchange rate does not mean a unique value at which the rate should remain. If economic conditions alter, the exchange rate policy modifies the foreign exchange rate as well.

The managed stability of the exchange rate grants more predictability to private investment. Entrepreneurs who pursue to export their products or need to import their inputs gain more stability in their ventures. Moreover, a stable exchange rate also means lesser foreign exchange risk at international investment. Notwithstanding the reduction of investment and business risks, a stable exchange rate also restrains the pass-through effect from exchange rate depreciations to domestic prices. In this sense, the exchange rate policy collaborates with monetary policy.

Exchange rate administration obliges countries to bear reserves in the specific foreign currency whose price is governed in terms of domestic currency. However, a country cannot, of course, produce another country's currency. To be able to administer the internal price of foreign currency (i.e., the exchange rate), the country must obtain this foreign currency by means of the current account and/ or the capital account of its balance of payment. In more technical parlance, to control the *price* of foreign currency, a country must have a *quantity* of this currency. This quantity is the country's foreign reserves, which it uses to balance the supply of, and demand for, foreign currency in the domestic exchange rate market; thereby, the exchange rate is administered. Hence, countries without reserves cannot administer their exchange rate.

Countries can secure reserves by means of surpluses in their balance of payments. These surpluses can result from positive trade and/or financial balances. With regard to financial flows, in the absence of controls over external capital, the exchange rate administration implies the use of the central bank's interest rate to deal with the attraction of foreign capital. But the base interest rate is a monetary policy tool whose use for foreign exchange affairs could remove autonomy from the central bank to manage domestic matters. For a sustainable exchange rate management, Keynes proposed controlling the international financial capital flows and the foreign exchange market. This control was to be set by a regulatory framework that would discriminate the type of and/or the conditions in which capital could enter or leave the country. Keynes explained the necessity to control external capital by saying that

> Shall we have to submit to exchange controls on individual transactions which would be unnecessary otherwise? . . . It is not merely a question of curbing exchange speculations and movements of hot money, or even of avoiding flights of capital due to political motives . . . the need, in my judgment, is more fundamental. Unless the aggregate of the new investments which individuals are free to make overseas is kept within the amount which our favourable trade balance is capable of looking after, we lose control over the domestic rate of interest.
>
> *(1980b, p. 275)*

The administration of the exchange rate will manage the level of the exchange rate and reduce its volatility; thus, the exchange rate policy minimizes investment risks caused by a chance-guided exchange rate. To not extract autonomy from monetary policy, the exchange rate policy must implement capital controls to handle financial capital flowing into or out of the country. But there remains a problem. If the country's trade balance is in deficit, it wastes foreign reserves in the world. Moreover, all countries cannot be in surplus at the same time (this would only be possible if planet earth could transact with other planets, which is impossible so far). How is it possible to manage the exchange rate if trade balance losses make countries miss the reserves with which they administer the exchange rate? Keynes' response to this question was also his utopia: the International Clearing Union.

The International Clearing Union

Keynes' position on international commerce changed throughout his life. As he was getting rather more concerned with production than prices, he left being a supporter of free trade to become its opponent – of course, his change also accompanied the downsizing of the British position in the global trade during the time of his life. Keynes' opposition to free trade was based on the fact that countries have different histories and natural resources. Hence, their places in global trade were unequal. Keynes did not believe in an economy self-regulated by markets. Thus, free trade would not organize the world economy and provide any country with a better productive structure; quite the opposite, free trade would strengthen disparities. In fact, Keynes' analysis is still true today. Some countries have trade balance surpluses while many do not, and the latter is the unjust counterpart of the former. But most importantly, the trade balance winners do not export only goods and services to the loser countries: they also export unemployment.

Having experienced the Versailles Treaty, Keynes saw how countries could guide their actions motivated by punitive sentiments instead of constructive feelings. Therefore, he disbelieved in the goodwill of international trade winner countries to voluntarily use their gains to balance the external deficits of the loser countries. In *A Treatise*, Keynes already analyzed the problems of international monetary management and made some considerations regarding the establishment of a supranational payment system. But it was at the United Nations Monetary and Financial Conference, held in Bretton Woods, USA, in 1944, that Keynes presented a major plan he had forged to restructure the international monetary and financial system after World War II.

A central piece in the so-called Keynes Plan was the International Clearing Union. Keynes planned this supranational and multilateral entity to automatically clear surpluses and deficits between countries in their external trade. The Clearing Union was a kind of international market maker in the sense that it would function to equilibrate their member countries' trade balance.

The ingenious Keynes Plan foresaw the creation of an international currency, the Bancor, issued by the International Clearing Union. This international currency had no role as a reserve of value, so it would be meaningless to accumulate it as a foreign reserve. The Bancor would only function as an international means of exchange. The Clearing Union would convert the gains of countries with surpluses in their trade balance in Bancor, which its holders could only use then to import from countries with deficit in their external trade. In the end, the International Clearing Union would clear the external trade balance of its member countries.

With the International Clearing Union in force, its member countries would not need to concern with wasting foreign reserves on the world through their external trade balance. Associated, the International Clearing Union plus controls over financial flows would, respectively, protect the current account balance and the capital account of the country's balance of payment. With the current and capital accounts taken care of, the management of foreign exchange by the exchange rate policy would become facilitated. The administered stability of the exchange rate could be more easily reached, and without threatening the autonomy that monetary policy requires to manage the central bank's base interest rate having domestic issues in sight. Unfortunately, there is no room in this book for detailing the Plan Keynes proposed and his participation in the 1944 Bretton Woods Conference. Detailed accounts of it can be seen in Steil (2013) and Carter (2020). In turn, Ferrari Filho (2006) explained the economics behind the Keynes Plan.

We briefly recounted Keynes' proposal for the exchange rate policy. This policy is the last of his economic policy propositions that we present. Monetary, fiscal (income policy included), and exchange rate policies form the scope of economic policies that Keynes required the State to perform to build macroeconomic stability and make the economy reach full employment and improved income distribution. In all these policies, stability is the keyword. The economy is too subject to fluctuations because of the subjective determinants of effective demand, namely, *propensity* to consume, *expectations* of prospective gains, and liquidity *preference*. To counterbalance and anchor these too subjective variables that determine effective demand, Keynes asked for State economic action. Monetary, fiscal, and exchange rate policies are the biggest part of such action. If Keynes demanded State to economically act, what did he say about the State? The next chapter replies to this question and presents Keynes' considerations about the State.

References

Carter, Z. D. (2020). *The Price of Peace: Money, Democracy and the Life of John Maynard Keynes*. New York: Random House.

Ferrari Filho, F. (2006). *Política Comercial, Taxa de Câmbio e Moeda Internacional – uma Análise a Partir de Keynes*. Porto Alegre: UFRGS.

Keynes, J. M. (1980b). *Activities 1940–1944: Shaping the Post-War world – The Clearing Union: The Collected Writings of John Maynard Keynes*, vol. XXV. London: Royal Economic Society and Cambridge University Press.

Keynes, J. M. (2013b). *A Treatise on Money I, the Pure Theory of Money: The Collected Writings of John Maynard Keynes*, vol. V. London: Cambridge University Press.

Keynes, J. M. (2013c). *A Treatise on Money II, the Applied Theory of Money: The Collected Writings of John Maynard Keynes*, vol. VI. London: Cambridge University Press.

Steil, B. (2013). *The Battle of Bretton Woods – John Maynard Keynes, Harry Dexter White and the Making of a New World Order*. Princeton, NJ: Princeton University Press.

16

THE STATE

Keynes continuously emphasized the key role that States can and should perform in the economy. He believed that economic stability would come with them, as they counterbalance and foster private initiative. This was the only way to achieve full employment and better income distribution. Proof of his belief in the State is that he worked with different British governments to help the United Kingdom confront major problems, like the 1914 and 1929 economic crises and World Wars I and II.

In July 1944, Keynes was the main delegate of the British commission, and the most notable person to take part in the Bretton Woods Conference, which formatted the international monetary and financial system after World War II. His proposals in the Conference defended that national States needed to structure a multilateral and supranational organization to coordinate the future global economy. He saw this State-based global economic coordination as the way to avoid disasters such as those that happened in between the two Great Wars.

Keynes also criticized States when they caused more harm than good. Both his aversion to totalitarian States, like Nazi Germany, Fascist Italy, and Stalinist-Communist Russia, and his protests against the reparations that the winner States imposed over Germany in the Versailles Treaty illustrate that Keynes did not take it for granted that States are always good.

Although State is everywhere in Keynes' claims, he did not write a theory of State. However, in some of his books, pamphlets, and articles, we can find pieces of a State structure that he sketched. This chapter explores three aspects of this sketch, namely, how Keynes expected the formation of State entities; the Agenda that he proposed for organizing the State economic action; and who he believed should be the staff members of State entities.[1]

In the 1925 pamphlet *Am I a Liberal?*, Keynes (2013e) pointed out that he expected that State entities could emerge from individuals' collective action, like a

DOI: 10.4324/9781003287094-21

bottom-to-top born entity. Inspired by joint-stock companies, whose ownership is collective as many individuals can own shares of them, Keynes believed that individuals could unite themselves and propose to the State the creation of its agencies. Keynes foresaw two benefits coming from this sort of creation of State entities. First, when loads of people make something, the result is impersonal as it cannot be taken as a one-person work. States, of course, could and should create their entities, but they must prevent these entities from being understood as the work of a single person. Keynes was against personalization of public things and trusted that collective action could impede it.

The second belief that Keynes held was that entities emerging from collective action would embed public spirit and welfare in State entities. The fact that individuals engage themselves in a cooperative movement to form State entities would reinforce these entities' public spirit, directed toward public welfare. Individuals would become concerned with reputation and create social habits that provide society with stability.

Keynes argued that these entities could be either State-owned or private–public partnerships – as for the latter, they are of especial importance in companies operating infrastructure, such as the case of the port of London, an example that Keynes (2013e) gave. Rest assured that public welfare is always preserved, the partnerships between public and private initiatives imply that both sectors constantly dialogue and cooperate with each other so that their interests match over time. Keynes was not attached to the private or public sector; he did not prefer one to the other; he preferred cooperation. Only with cooperation, guided to public welfare, the economy would find the stability it needs to reach full employment and better income distribution.

Keynes talked about semi-autonomy for State entities. By semi-autonomy, he meant that these entities should have partial autonomy in relation to other State bodies, including the parliament and government. At the same time, semi also signifies that these entities need to be, partly, under the control of the parliament and government. Notice that Keynes' proposal created a kind of tension between State entities, governors, and congresspeople. He valued this tension because it could strengthen the character impersonal of State agencies. Semi-autonomy makes them subordinated to but concomitantly protected from the politicians occupying the parliament and government of the day.

To organize the State economic action, Keynes proposed what he called Agenda, which appeared in *Am I a Liberal?* (Keynes, 2013e). The Agenda is an idea to synthesize all economic fronts in which the State acts. It comprises the State economic actors and economic policies. Hence, monetary, fiscal, and exchange rate policies, the semi-autonomous economic State entities, as well as the capital budget, its investment, and technically social works are all components of the Agenda.

The Agenda shows Keynes' preoccupation with the durability of State economic actions. The measures enrolled in the Agenda should last over time. They are not a government thing only; they should not be replaced as fast as governments and congresspeople change. Obviously, constituents present new desires and needs whenever they vote. However, what people long for must not replace everything that was in force from the past.

Keynes idealized the Agenda to combine and manage old policies with the fresh policies that were chosen by the people when they democratically elected a government. One task of the agenda is to make new and old policies coexist for as long as they create public welfare. Old policies will end when their effects no longer justify their existence and new ones will occupy the Agenda. But the idea of the Agenda came into Keynes' mind to avoid strong and fast ruptures. As this book insistently buzzed, the determinants of effective demand are too prone to abrupt changes as they are too subjective. Propensity, preference, and expectations are inclined to rapid shifts whose direct effect is on economic activity.

Hence, the Agenda is a State element that Keynes proposed for economies to pursue their long-term stability. By means of both the concrete actions it undertakes and the information it produces, the Agenda anchors individuals' opinions about what they should expect for the future. It is not an insurance against economic cycles because such a thing cannot exist as cannot exist a thing that prevents humans from changing their humor according to the news. However, the Agenda makes State action stable, therefore individuals' changeable mood should not expect instabilities from the government at least.

The staff members that form State bureaucracy should be people, following Keynes (2013e), who carry public spirit, ambition, and technical knowledge. They are responsible for actualizing the Agenda, which is not an easy task. Hence, Keynes proposed this technocratic, almost aristocratic, profile of workers to administer State entities and operate their actions. These members of staff are not responsible for selecting *which* policy should be done; it is society that decides when people voted and elected candidates. Staff members account for *how* to implement a policy. Insofar as such implementation involves technical challenges, Keynes suggested that technical people should take care of it. Moreover, State entities' semi-autonomy also contributes to the implementation of the economic actions that these entities are responsible for because it grants instrumental autonomy to their staff members. The bureaucracy can try to achieve the policies that people have voted for when they elected their political representation without being harassed by external influences who seek to attend to their personal interests.

Nevertheless, the State is not solely responsible for economic actions. It handles these actions, but its functions go well beyond economic matters. Keynes saw the State as the great social peacemaker. The State is a kind of a big table where all social agents sit to complain about their discomforts and claim their desires. The State is the big conciliator of free societies. It shapes itself in the form needed to avoid the eruption of conflicts that can threaten individual liberty. Economies are part of what States need to pay attention to make peace prevail; it may be a big part of peacemaking because capitalism has made almost everything tradeable. Yet, economics is not everything.

If the State is not this big conciliator that Keynes trusted it could be, it can be either nothing or everything. Those who believe in the *laissez-faire* invisible hand of markets want the minimal State, especially in economic matters, in which the government should do nothing but, at most, help the market to solve its failures. In turn, those who dislike the vast economic freedom of individuals favor large State economic control; they hold the belief that the State is everything. Keynes was on neither of these sides but in the midpoint between them, because neither him in his time, us in ours, nor capitalism since its beginning, saw markets or States alone reaching full employment and eliminating inequality. Private initiative and States can transform individual freedom into collective action to jointly forge the path of society toward social, economic, and human development. Keynes had an image of what he foresaw as the developed stage of society. The next chapter presents it.

Note

1 Much of the research that based this chapter and the next one was previously and originally done by me and my dear friends and professors Fernando Ferrari Filho and Pedro Cezar Dutra Fonseca and was published in Terra, Ferrari Filho, and Fonseca (2021).

References

Keynes, J. M. (2013e). *Essays in Persuasion (Am I a Liberal?) The Collected Writings of John Maynard Keynes*, vol. IX. London: Royal Economic Society and Cambridge University Press.

Terra, F. H. B., Ferrari Filho, F. and Fonseca, P. C. D. (2021). 'Keynes on State and Economic Development', *Review of Political Economy*, 33(1), pp. 88–102. DOI: 10.1080/09538259.2020.1823072.

17

DEVELOPMENT

Development is a discipline of economics that investigates the conditions required for both structurally improving the productive and distributional conditions of countries and permanently enhancing people's life quality in objective and subjective terms. Development is associated with quantitative GDP growth because in the absence of growth, the task of developing a country becomes harder as the distributive conflict in the economy intensifies. Still, GDP growth is not synonymous with development and both concepts should not be confused; the former is, in general, a necessary but not a sufficient condition for development.

You can think of, for example, environmental, economic, and social development, but the noun *development* has gained so much importance in the last decades that its use without an adjective qualifying it will bear meaning to economists – surely different meanings because economists mostly agree to disagree. Terra, Ferrari Filho, and Fonseca (2021) pointed out that the specific concept of economic development, meaning structural productive and distributive changes in the economy accompanied by improvements in people's standard of living, appeared in the 1950s. Human development, a well-known index that is partially composed of an economic indicator, grew strong in the passage of the 1980s to the 1990s.

Thus, development as an autonomous topic of research in economics came after Keynes passed away in 1946. However, running through his works and bearing in mind that development means structural economic changes which permanently enhance people's quality of life, we can gather pieces of what Keynes expected for the future of society and draw his notion of development. This notion might sound strange to the eyes and ears of today's experts on development, but it should be remembered that Keynes lived before the definitions of the boundaries circumscribing what is currently understood by this term. Lest you do not get surprised or bored with the following lines, we remind you that Keynes saw economics as a moral science, dealing with the moral codes that drive human behavior. Therefore,

DOI: 10.4324/9781003287094-22

do not get startled if you feel that economic variables play little role in Keynes' notion of development. If you feel that while reading the following pages, you are getting Keynes right.

Development in Keynes is a historical stage, a sort of arrival point that he wished societies to reach in the course of their history. He suggested macroeconomic policies and the Agenda as means to stabilize the economy which, in turn, is necessary for solving the two biggest economic problems of monetary economies of production, namely, involuntary unemployment and unequal wealth and income distribution. Nevertheless, the economy will not see development just because its greatest problems were solved. These were, Keynes believed, short-term maladjustments that have been always present in the economy because until his time economics had not yet furnished the right tools to solve them properly. But in the long run, after the maladjustments were solved, society would construct a historical stage in which "the economic problem is not – if we look into the future – *the problem of the human race*" (Keynes, 2013e, p. 326, marks in the original).

Wars come and go, and natural disasters, too; they are dreadful events that occasionally occur. But the economic disaster, which means people struggling for survival, dying from starvation, borrowing money to pay for the basic needs of life, becoming homeless and/or unable to get decent jobs, and so forth has been permanent in history. Economic problems have been the continuing pandemic of capitalism. But strangely, no vaccine has been developed for it; countries seem to have gotten accustomed to the economic disease despite its nefarious effects on people. Full employment and better income distribution, both accomplished by the association of the private and public sectors in favor of overcoming the economic disease that daily sickens people's life, would be a necessary juncture before the final stage of development.

Having surpassed the economic problems of everyday life, the next stage is development. In Keynes' words, in this developed stage, people would "cultivate into a fuller perfection, the art of life itself and do not sell themselves for the means of life, who will be able to enjoy the abundance when it comes" (2013e, p. 328). Moreover, Keynes envisioned

> for the first time since his creation man will be faced with his real permanent problem – how to use his freedom from pressing economic cares, how to occupy the leisure, which science and compound interest will have won for him, to live wisely and agreeably and well.
>
> *(2013e, p. 328)*

A life to live, not to struggle with economic questions: this was Keynes' view of development.

You can be thinking right now that Keynes' view was way too idealistic to become effective. But the question is not about being idealistic. The problem is the moral code that sustains people's ideals. The neoclassical economists who believe in the invisible hands of markets are driven by ideals whose base is on their moral codes. Revolutionary people who do not mind going to war to reach their utopia have their ideals in accordance with their moral codes. Keynes, too, had his moral code; not for less, he suggested moral principles to persuade people about the ideals that sustained his economics.

As Chapter 12 showed, after 23 chapters of pure economics, the grand finale Keynes chose to end his *The General Theory* was not economics, but social philosophy. He offered a new economic theory that changed the comprehension of how the economy really works. Accordingly, he also delivered a new moral code aimed at changing people's economic attitudes. If only his new economics had arisen, people would still live by the moral code of the past. Thus, all his effort to deliver a different comprehension of the economy, to recognize its real problems, their causes, and solutions would be condemned to failure.

Nevertheless, Keynes' moral code is exclusive neither to *The General Theory* nor to his major economic works. It was everywhere in his life: in *The Nation and The Athenaeum* (the liberal newspaper he bought in 1923), in his extensive production of public opinion articles, in his patronage of arts throughout his life, in his friendship with the Bloomsbury group and their battle against the conservative habits of society, in his abandonment of the Versailles Treaty for the reasons he publicly exposed in *The Economic Consequences of the Peace*, and in his participation in the Bretton Woods Conference, despite of being in such a weak health condition that he died in 1946, shortly after the final agreement of Bretton Woods was signed, in Savannah, USA, in March that year, among many other examples.

In his moral crusade, Keynes strongly battled against what he called love of money. Instead of working and producing to live life well, individuals, especially the wealthiest ones, have confused means with ends. They directed their lives to accumulate money instead of using money as means to enjoy life. These individuals had already gained enough to afford their material independence, but they nevertheless got dependent on gaining money uninterruptedly.

The liquidity fetish of wealthy people has worsened with the advent of financialization and made their love of money utter. Not only are individuals compelled by the motto of money accumulation, but also are they financially investing their money on unproductive assets for the sake of fulfilling their love of accumulating. This means that society has rewarded and made rich individuals that time ago agreed to confront the risks of uncertainty and invested their loved money on productive capital assets. But these same people have accumulated money and now prefer to satisfy their love for mounting money by mostly investing it on financial assets, which only devolves to society a small portion of what society has first provided these accumulators with.

Keynes praised individual freedom and private initiative so much that his major intentions sought to preserve it at most, especially because his time surrounded him with experiences that have withdrawn people's liberty, either World Wars or capitalistic and non-capitalistic social regimes. Such was the high-ranked position of individual liberty in his moral code that among the innumerous economic, political, and social proposals that Keynes made, he never suggested the prohibition of money accumulation. If people wanted that, they could have it. He tried to illuminate people about love of money's negative effects on productive investment, employment, economic activity, and distribution by showing them that there could exist an economy where people depended on accumulating money only to the extent that their material needs for a joyful life required.

Keynes' position has nothing to do with everyone living with just a few. Each country and each culture within each country know what enough means. Keynes' ideal was to convey society to a developed stage in which money no longer affects people by its effects on either most of society who struggle for subsisting or affect those few rich individuals whose lives were enslaved by their love of money's unstoppable desire for accumulating money for the sake of nothing but money accumulation itself.

Keynes questioned that the motto of capitalism was love of money instead of love of living. Hence, he tried to convince people that joy rather than money accumulation could fulfill the emptiness of a non-fated existence, such as ours. It is a duty of great intellectuals to offer ideals and ways to make ideals reality. Keynes fulfilled this task.

In Keynes' terms, development is the historical stage of society in which the short-term maladjustments have been overcome, the material needs of people were satisfied, and love of living has substituted love of money as the motto of individual economic behavior. Keynes theorized his economics to show that money is not neutral to economics; the course of the economy changes whether people spend money to consume, or invest it, or hold it preferring its absolute liquidity to any degree of illiquidity. He proposed economic policies and the Agenda to stabilize the economy against the cycles that confront society occasionally as people change their expectations and opinions and, finally, their holdings of money. He offered a moral code to show that the problem is not money itself as critics could wrongly conclude, but how people's minds got accustomed to use it as an object of desire and not as an object to realize desires.

References

Keynes, J. M. (2012). *The Economic Consequences of the Peace*. Summit: Start Publishing.

Keynes, J. M. (2013d). *The General Theory of Employment, Interest and Money: The Collected Writings of John Maynard Keynes*, vol. VII. London: Royal Economic Society and Cambridge University Press.

Keynes, J. M. (2013e). *Essays in Persuasion*, vol. IX. London: Royal Economic Society and Cambridge University Press.

Terra, F. H. B., Ferrari Filho, F. and Fonseca, P. C. D. (2021). 'Keynes on State and Economic Development', *Review of Political Economy*, 33(1), pp. 88–102. DOI: 10.1080/09538259.2020.1823072.

CONCLUSION

The main intention of those who venture to draft a book is to pass a certain message to readers. Obviously, that is the intention of this book, too. We have traveled a long road on the work of John Maynard Keynes. We started in his *A Treatise on Probability*, which he wrote in the 1900s, and arrived at the economic proposals of his late life, such as his prescriptions for fiscal, monetary, and exchange rate policies, which he mostly advanced in the 1940s. Now, at the end of our journey, it is time to reiterate the message this book intended you to hear: the economics of John Maynard Keynes are still valid in a world that has never really been able to combat its economic problems. The problems that cause anger, discontent, delusion, and other banes of humanity have multifold causes. It will not be economists who will solve them. But economists can help in the battle if they extricate the economy from the several issues that beset humans. This was Keynes' message.

Keynes' path on economics was winding. Fortunately, he did not finish his life holding the same beliefs he had had in his youth; this is fortunate because by confronting his own belief in neoclassical economics, a theory that he had been taught and he later lectured, he could do economics his way. By doing economics his way, Keynes bequeathed to the world his surname to form both the adjective Keynesian and the noun Keynesianism. However, the meaning of both terms is frequently wrongly taken, especially by critics who try to associate Keynes with expansionary fiscal policy that pursues GDP growth and low unemployment regardless of cost, especially inflation. We hope that this book has made it clear that this Keynesianism is not Keynesian. We quoted Keynes himself at length to leave you in no doubt as to his economics and their meaning.

Keynes is still much recalled. However, this remembrance only happens because, every now and then, recession captures the economy and, when it does, the opportunistic Keynesianism calls for bigger State economic action. But Keynes was about much more than saving the economy from crises; in fact, he tried to prevent crises.

DOI: 10.4324/9781003287094-23

Not only did he realize that economic crises had more than just economic effects, but he also saw the impacts of these non-economic effects on history in his lifetime. Keynes lived in a hectic world that passed through World War I, the interwar period, the Great Depression, Fascism, Nazism, Stalinism, and World War II. He saw his country, the United Kingdom, lose its dominant place in the world. These events caused the winding course of his ideas.

A century after Keynes, these 2010s and 2020s have been strange times too. Who would have bet on Europe taking a step back in its unification with Brexit in 2016, when the United Kingdom, a country that is itself a union of countries, left the European Union? Who would have anticipated that from 2019 to 2021 the world would endure one and a half years of social distancing because of a pandemic? Who could have imagined a mob invading the US Capitol in 2021? Who would have believed in a Russian invasion of Ukraine in 2022 and a months-long war breaking out in continental Europe? Who would have guessed that democracy would be in danger in Brazil in 2022? Who could have imagined a candidate for prime minister in Japan being assassinated in that country's 2022 electoral run?

In all these exceptional circumstances, the economy has played a role. It is not the whole problem, but it has been an ongoing part of the problem, with its crises, its inability to create jobs and to distribute wealth, its resignation to poverty, its incapacity to build multilateral decisions as quickly as is necessary to repair the environmental destruction. And things have been worsened by the fact that modern sociability has created and sustained the illusion that individual initiative is more important than society. This new outlook started in the 1970s with the end of the post-War policies, upon which Keynes had had so much influence as he attempted to build a world that could see itself as one. It must not be forgotten that Keynes proposed his economics to save private individual initiative from totalitarian regimes. However, he saw society as never reducible to the mere sum of individuals; society is obviously an outcome of individual initiative, but where one plus one equals three, maybe five.

When an entrepreneur sells, there is a worker, who may even be unemployed, buying. When a worker is hired, there is an entrepreneur contracting. Inputs that a seller vended yesterday are today an output that another producer manufactured aiming at selling it to a consumer tomorrow. The economy can never be a one-person thing. It is inevitably a social thing; thus, it can never be left on the shoulders of individuals alone. This explains why States are so important in Keynes' view.

States exist to defend and secure public interests. However, when they do so, they regulate what individuals can and cannot do, and thus they limit individual initiative. Moreover, States tax and spend, promoting income redistribution between individuals. One way or another, State actions touch on individual initiative. However, this touch has increasingly contradicted modern sociability whose logic is that the individual is more important than society. Therefore, any State touch in individual initiative has been deemed bad, as illustrated by slogans you often hear, such as taxes are robbery, State economic intervention is an inefficiency creator, or compulsory vaccination, a part of States' public health strategy, is a crime against individual freedom. This happened before and during Keynes' time as well. He was aware of how thirsty for power individuals can be. His economics acknowledged this, for instance, in the roles of both the entrepreneur and consumer; the bottom-to-top born State entities; democracy as means for individuals to choose what they want; and the State modulation of economic cycles to avoid crises that could threaten the individual liberty on which capitalism is based.

But Keynes did not experience in his time, nor did we in ours, free markets solving involuntary unemployment and unequal income distribution. Because the repercussions of economic crises go well beyond economic matters and free markets do not guarantee the solution of the problems ever troubling the economy, in the end, free markets can greatly threaten individual liberty. It is a shame that after so long fervent individual liberty and free market's believers have not yet seen that Keynes questioned the latter to save the former and stated that the State could act as the great propeller of private initiative. Keynes saw the individual within society and not society within the individual. In this sense, he was trying to revolutionize capitalism without running the risk of imploding it.

Keynes fought for his belief that the world could be a better place and life could be joyfully lived. He believed in the power of reason to battle wrong ideas and to manage human progress. In his later life, Keynes became quite dismayed at the use mankind was making of its power to reason, as he expressed in his 1938 text *My Early Beliefs* (Keynes, 2013f). Yet he never stopped fighting for his ideal of a better life lived in a better world. His efforts were very fruitful, yet less fruitful than they could have been if his economic theory and economic proposals were implemented.

Keynes' legacy is immense. Take, for example, Milton Friedman, a major economist of the 20th Century. He broadly contested Keynes' ideas, but he did so using themes whose importance Keynes has brought to economics, such as expectations, monetary policy, unemployment and the consumption function. Had Keynes not developed these themes, what would have Friedman focused on? Moreover, Keynes' economics is so intriguing that those who affiliate with neoclassical economics (or other perspectives it inspired) see Keynes almost as Karl Marx; however, those who follow Karl Marx see Keynes almost as neoclassical. Neither there, nor here; John Maynard Keynes was always himself and let us hope this book has made that irreducibly and convincingly clear.

References

Keynes, J. M. (1921). *A Treatise on Probability*. London: Macmillan.

Keynes, J. M. (2013f). *Essays in Biography (My Early Beliefs), the Collected Writings of John Maynard Keynes*, vol. X. London: Royal Economic Society and Cambridge University Press.

BIBLIOGRAPHICAL REFERENCES

Bateman, B. W. (1989). '"Human Logic" and Keynes' Economics: A Comment', *Eastern Economic Journal*, 15(1), pp. 63–67.

Bateman, B. W. (1991). 'Das Maynard Keynes Problem', *Cambridge Journal of Economics*, 15(1), pp. 100–111.

Biböw, J. (2002). 'Keynes on Central Banking and the Structure of Monetary Policy', *History of Political Economy*, 34(4), pp. 749–787.

Carter, Z. D. (2020). *The Price of Peace: Money, Democracy and the Life of John Maynard Keynes*. New York: Random House.

Carvalho, F. J. C. (1988). 'Keynes on Probability, Uncertainty and Decision Making', *Journal of Post-Keynesian Economics*, 11(1), pp. 66–81.

Carvalho, F. J. C. (1992). *Mr. Keynes and the Post Keynesians*. Cheltenham: Edward Elgar.

Carvalho, F. J. C. (2003). 'Características Essenciais do Método de Keynes na Teoria Geral', in Corazza, G. (ed.) *Métodos da Ciência Econômica*. Porto Alegre: UFRGS, pp. 175–188.

Carvalho, F. J. C. (2015). 'Keynes on Expectations, Uncertainty and Defensive Behavior', *Brazilian Keynesian Review*, 1(1), pp. 44–54.

Colander, D. (1984). 'Was Keynes a Keynesian or a Lernerian?', *Journal of Economic Literature*, 22(4), pp. 1572–1575.

Ferrari Filho, F. (2006). *Política Comercial, Taxa de Câmbio e Moeda Internacional – uma Análise a Partir de Keynes*. Porto Alegre: UFRGS.

Ferrari-Filho, F. and Conceição, O. A. C. (2005). 'The Concept of Uncertainty in Post Keynesian and in Institutional Economics', *Journal of Economic Issues*, 39(3), pp. 579–594. DOI: 10.1080/00213624.2005.11506835.

Friedman, M. (1953). *Essays in Positive Economics*. Chicago: University of Chicago Press.

Hesse, M. (1987). 'Keynes and the Method of Analogy', *Topoi*, 6(1), pp. 65–74.

Keynes, J. M. (1913). *Indian Currency and Finance*. London: Macmillan.

Keynes, J. M. (1921). *A Treatise on Probability*. London: Macmillan.

Keynes, J. M. (1936). 'Fluctuations in Net Investment in the United States', *Economic Journal*, 46(183), pp. 540–547.

Keynes, J. M. (1973). *The General Theory and After: Part I Preparation. The Collected Writings of John Maynard Keynes*, vol. XIII. London: Royal Economic Society and Macmillan.

Keynes, J. M. (1980a). *Activities 1940–1946: Shaping the Post-War World – Employment and Commodities. The Collected Writings of John Maynard Keynes*, vol. XXVII. London: Royal Economic Society and Macmillan.

Keynes, J. M. (1980b). *Activities 1940–1944: Shaping the Post-War World – The Clearing Union. The Collected Writings of John Maynard Keynes*, vol. XXV. London: Royal Economic Society and Cambridge University Press.

Keynes, J. M. (1982). *Activities 1931–1939 World Crises and Policies in America and Britain (The Monetary Policy of the Labour Party): The Collected Writings of John Maynard Keynes*, vol. XXI. London: Royal Economic Society and Cambridge University Press.

Keynes, J. M. (2012). *The Economic Consequences of the Peace*. Summit: Start Publishing.

Keynes, J. M. (2013a). *A Tract on Monetary Reform: The Collected Writings of John Maynard Keynes*, vol. IV. London: Cambridge University Press.

Keynes, J. M. (2013b). *A Treatise on Money I, the Pure Theory of Money: The Collected Writings of John Maynard Keynes*, vol. V. London: Cambridge University Press.

Keynes, J. M. (2013c). *A Treatise on Money II, the Applied Theory of Money: The Collected Writings of John Maynard Keynes*, vol. VI. London: Cambridge University Press.

Keynes, J. M. (2013d). *The General Theory of Employment, Interest and Money: The Collected Writings of John Maynard Keynes*, vol. VII. London: Royal Economic Society and Cambridge University Press.

Keynes, J. M. (2013e). *Essays in Persuasion (Am I a Liberal?), the Collected Writings of John Maynard Keynes*, vol. IX. London: Royal Economic Society and Cambridge University Press.

Keynes, J. M. (2013f). *Essays in Biography, the Collected Writings of John Maynard Keynes*, vol. X. London: Royal Economic Society and Cambridge University Press.

Kregel, J. (1985). 'Budget Deficits, Stabilisation Policy and Liquidity Preference: Keynes's Post-War Policy Proposals', in Vicarelli, F. (ed.) *Keynes's Relevance Today*. London: Macmillan, pp. 28–50.

Lerner, A. (1943). 'Functional Finance and the Federal Debt', *Social Research*, 10(1), pp. 38–51.

Minsky, H. (1986). *Stabilizing an Unstable Economy*. A Twentieth Century Fund Report. New Haven: Yale University Press.

O'Donnell, R. M. (1989). *Keynes: Philosophy, Economics and Politics*. New York: St. Martin's Press.

O'Donnell, R. M. (2002). *The Thick and the Thin of Controversy: A Critique of Bateman on Keynes*. Research Papers 0204. Sydney: Macquarie University, Department of Economics.

Pigou, A. C. (1933). *The Theory of Employment*. London: Macmillan.

Russell, B. (1912). *The Problems of Philosophy*. New York: Henry Holt and Company.

Scazzieri, R. (2021). 'Patterning Uncertainty: Partial Likeness, Analogy and Likelihood', *Cambridge Journal of Economics*, 45, pp. 1009–1026.

Shackle, G. L. S. (1979). *Imagination and the Nature of Choice*. Edinburgh: Edinburgh University Press.

Steil, B. (2013). *The Battle of Bretton Woods – John Maynard Keynes, Harry Dexter White and the Making of a New World Order*. Princeton, NJ: Princeton University Press.

Terra, F. H. B. and Ferrari Filho, F. (2018). 'Reflections on Keynes' Method', *Revista Venezolana de Análisis de Coyuntura*, 24(1), pp. 85–101.

Terra, F. H. B., Ferrari Filho, F. and Fonseca, P. C. D. 'Keynes on State and Economic Development', *Review of Political Economy*, 33(1), pp. 88–102. DOI: 10.1080/09538259.2020.1823072.

Toneto, R., Ribas, T. and Carvalho, L. (2021). *Nota de Economia Política do MADE*. Centro de Pesquisa em Macroeconomia das Desigualdades, 008. São Paulo: MADE-Universidade de são Paulo.

Vercelli, A. (2010). *Weight of Argument and Economic Decisions.* Department of Economic Policy, Finance and Development (DEPFID), 0610. Siena: Department of Economic Policy, Finance and Development (DEPFID) of the Siena University.

Winslow, E. G. (1986). ' "Human Logic" and Keynes' Economics', *Eastern Economic Journal,* 12(4), pp. 413–430.

Winslow, E. G. (1989). ' "Human Logic" and Keynes' Economics: A Reply to Bateman', *Eastern Economic Journal,* 15(1), pp. 67–70.

INDEX

Printed in the United States
by Baker & Taylor Publisher Services